Sōshitsu Sen XVI

Urasenke Tea Procedure Guidebook 3

Koicha Tea Procedure

Furo Koicha Temae
Ro Koicha Temae
Knowledge for Guests

TANKOSHA

Technical Remarks

The romanization of Japanese is according to the Hepburn system. Long vowels in the Japanese words are indicated by a macron (¯), except in the case of words already known by an alternate spelling (e.g., noh) and place names which are widely known (e.g., Kyoto). Hyphenation is used sparingly to indicate the word elements in Japanese compound terms.

This English-language guidebook necessarily includes a large number of Japanese terms, for there are so many terms used in chadō which do not have English counterparts; among them, some of the most basic and common terms. Concerning the italicization of Japanese terms in this book, the most basic chadō terms are treated as English loanwords, and therefore are not italicized. In most cases, Japanese terms are defined in parentheses on first appearance. Also, a glossary of most of the terms is provided at the back.

Throughout this book, names of people are given in the order that is customary in the person's native country. The exception is the author's name on the title page, on the jacket and spine, and in the copyright information. Here the names are given in accordance with the international standards used in libraries and bookstores.

Urasenke Tea Procedure Guidebook 3
Koicha Tea Procedure

This book is a translation of the Japanese guidebook *Urasenke Chadō Temae Kyōsoku 3* authored by Sōshitsu Sen XVI and published by Tankosha Publishing Co., Ltd. on December 18, 2010.

Published on April 3, 2019, by Tankosha Publishing Co., Ltd., Kyoto.

© 2019 by Sōshitsu Sen, Chairman, Urasenke Foundation
All rights reserved

English translation
    Urasenke Tankokai Federation International Affairs Department
    (Gretchen Mittwer and Michael Hardy)

Photographs
    Masaki Miyano

Additional contributions
    Yukiyo Daido (page 124 insert photograph), Hideko Nakagawa (page 6 circled drawing), Michael Hardy (page 6 right column and page 21 illustrations)

Design
    Sein Inc., Kyoto

Printing and binding
    Dai Nippon Printing Co., Ltd.
Printed in Japan
ISBN978-4-473-04290-3

Urasenke Tea Procedure
Guidebook 3
Table of Contents

Introduction   4

Furo Koicha Temae   5

    Diagrams of Chaire and Shifuku   6

    The Preparations   7

Furo Koicha Temae   8

Ro Koicha Temae   61

    The Preparations   62

Ro Koicha Temae   63

Knowledge for Guests   123

Partaking of Koicha   124

Haiken **of the Chaire, Chashaku, and Shifuku**   139

How to Partake of Confections Served in a Fuchidaka   145

Glossary   150

Introduction

In chadō, the phrase "*ocha ippuku*" (a serving of tea) nearly automatically indicates a serving of koicha, matcha of thick consistency. Hence, the use of this phrase in an invitation to tea indicates that the event will be a *chaji*; that is, it will be a tea function surrounding the serving and drinking of koicha.

Within the context of a conventional, full chaji, the seating in which the serving of koicha takes place is preceded by the guests' initial seating (*shoiri*), before the room has been prepared for the koicha temae. During the *shoiri*, there is the host's building of the charcoal fire for heating the water to be used for the koicha temae, the serving of a *kaiseki* meal, and the serving of a moist, rather substantial type of confection referred to as "omogashi" (lit., main confection). After an intermission (*nakadachi*), the guests are called back to the tea room for the koicha, which is the climax of a chaji. For koicha, the amount of tea for the number of guests is prepared in a single bowl, and this is passed from guest to guest, each taking three-and-a-half sips. Generally, among all the implements used during a chaji, the highest importance is placed upon those used for the koicha service. The atmosphere is deliberate, quiet, and introspective. As a means of unifying the participants and space, the sadōguchi is closed during the temae, even in the warmer months of the furo season. Once the koicha temae ends, there is the replenishing of the charcoal fire, and finally comes the usucha service, when the atmosphere lightens up.

At tea plantations, delicate care goes into growing the tea used for koicha, to ensure the best possible aroma and flavor. Good quality new leaf sprouts are best, and a covering is spread above the plantation, to adjust the amount of direct sunlight reaching the bushes. Koicha is not made frothy like usucha, but rather, is made by blending the tea powder together with the hot water. The tea powder quantity, temperature and amount of hot water, and how well the blending is done are the three vital points in preparing a bowl of koicha.

To conduct a koicha temae requires deep, rigorous mental preparation and proper temae training.

Furo Koicha Temae

Diagrams of Chaire and Shifuku

Parts of the chaire and shifuku

Chaire
jar for powdered koicha

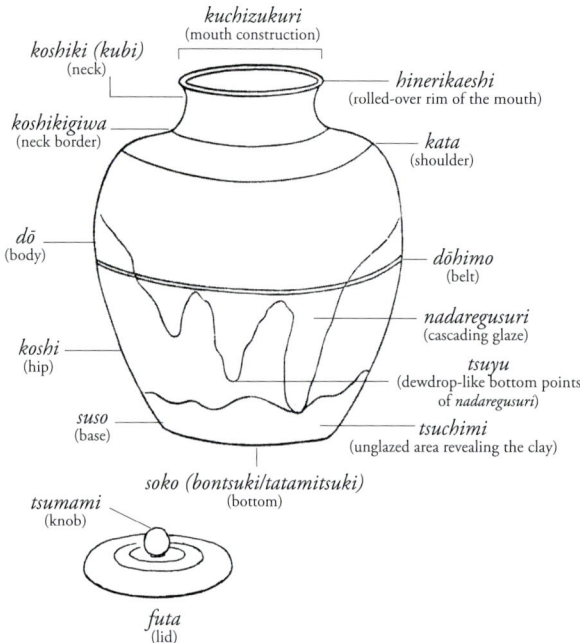

Shifuku
cloth pouch

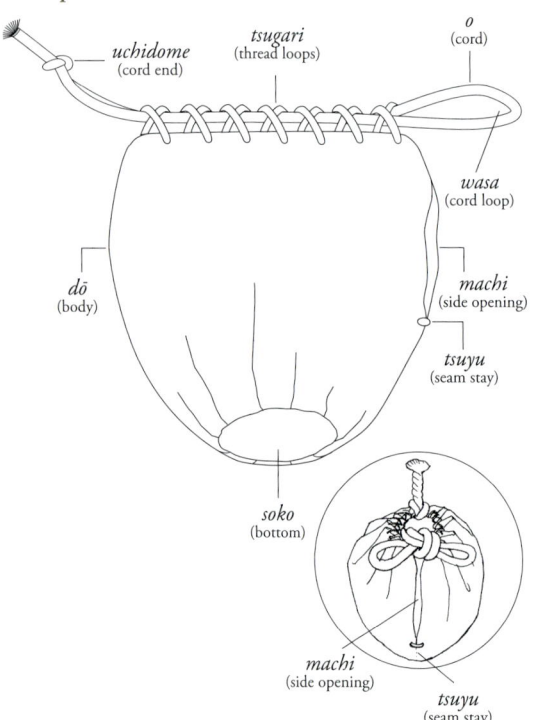

How to tie the shifuku cord

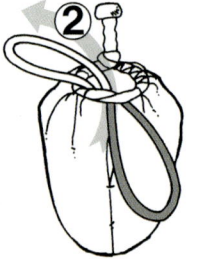

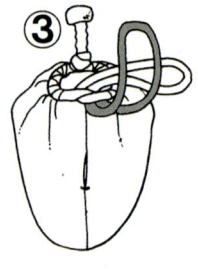

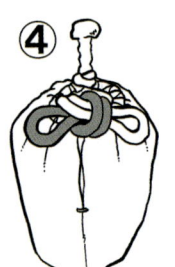

The Preparations

Generally, in the case of a spacious tea room (*hiroma*), place a short folding screen referred to as a *furosakibyōbu* in the corner on the *kattetsuki* side (the side closer to the mizuya) at the far end of the temaedatami, to set off the so-called implement mat (*dōgudatami*). Then place the *shikiita* (board onto which the furo is placed) on the *kattetsuki* side of the temaedatami. The standard positioning is 16 tatami weaves (*tatami-me*), or approximately 24 cm, up from the imaginary line extending from the inner side of the front bordering of the adjacent tatami for high-ranking personage's seating (*kinindatami*) and 7–9 tatami weaves, or approximately 10.5–13.5 cm, from the bordering on the *kattetsuki* side of the temaedatami. Next, rest the furo on the center of the *shikiita* and, after arranging the charcoal in the furo so that the fire begins to burn, rest the kettle on the trivet (*gotoku*) in the furo, and set the lid ajar so that the kettle mouth is open a crack at the back. In resting the kettle on the trivet, take care that it is evenly balanced. The line referred to as the *haochi* (lit., flange fallen away) around the lower part of the kettle, or the shoulder balance of the kettle, can be used as guides.

Fill the mizusashi with water to about 80%, and place it on the temaedatami so that its center is aligned with the kettle lugs and is midpoint on the right half of the temaedatami. Put enough powdered tea into the chaire (ceramic jar for koicha powder) for the number of guests, figuring on three heaping chashaku scoops, or 3.75 grams, per person. Then place the chaire inside its shifuku (cloth pouch) and tie the cord. See "How to tie the shifuku cord" diagrams on facing page. Place the so-readied chaire in front of the mizusashi on the temaedatami.

Have the chawan (set up with the chakin and chasen in it and chashaku resting face down across the right) and kensui (set up with the futaoki in it and furo-use hishaku face down across the top with its cup resting on the rim) ready in the mizuya. Remember to hang your fukusa from your obi and put your sensu aside.

The following temae is presented in a conventional type of 8-tatami *hiroma* having a straight forward sadōguchi (host's doorway). A sadōguchi in this position is referred to as a *shōmen-* or *tsukkomi-sadōguchi*.

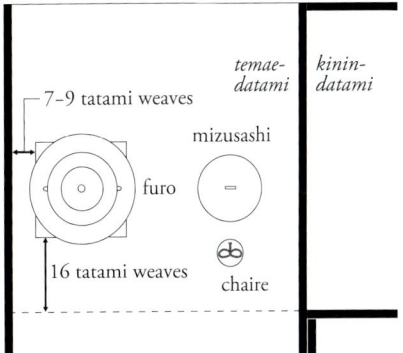

Carrying out the tea implements

Sit at the closed sadōguchi so that your knees are approximately 16 tatami weaves, or 24 cm, from the threshold, and place the chawan in front of your knees. Open the fusuma (1). Pick up the chawan with your right hand (2), place it in your left palm, and steady it with your right hand. Bring your right foot forward slightly (3), and stand up. To enter, cross the threshold with your right foot (4), walk along the center of the tatami, cross into the temaedatami with your right foot (5), proceed to the temaeza, and sit at the left-right center of the temaeza so that your knees are at the halfway point of the temaedatami (6). [Note: This seating position is the *teiza* or "standard seat" for doing furo temae in a conventional type of *hiroma*, as is being done here.]

Grasp the chawan from the right side with your right hand (7), hold it from the left-front with your left hand, and set it down on the *kattetsuki* side of the temaeza (8).

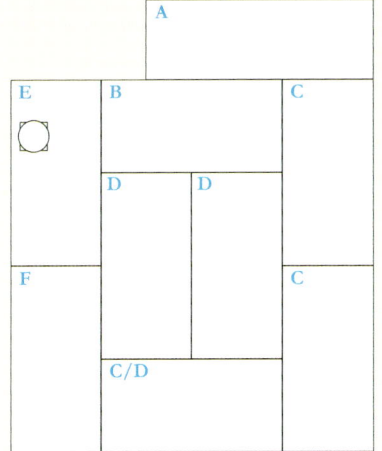

A Alcove / *Tokonoma*
  (Alcove mat / *Tokodatami*)
B High ranking personage's seating / *Kinindatami*
C Guests' seating / *Kyakudatami*
D Traversing mat / *Kayoidatami*
E Temae mat / *Temaedatami*
  (Implement mat / *Dōgudatami*)
F Host's entry mat / *Fumikomidatami*

The functional names of the tatami mats in a standard 8-tatami *hiroma* with furo

Footwork when entering with the chawan

sadōguchi

Pick up the clothed chaire with your right hand, and move it to the front right of the mizusashi (9). Pick up the chawan from the left-front with your left hand (10), hold it from the right side with your right hand (11), re-hold it from the side with your left hand, and place it to the front left of the mizusashi (12). Bring your left foot forward slightly, stand, turn in the direction of the guests, and return to the mizuya, making all the tatami-to-tatami cross-overs with your left foot.

Holding the prepared kensui with your left hand, enter the tea room from your right foot (13), turn your left foot inward and step in front of your right foot, bring the heel of your right foot around to point that foot in the direction of the sadōguchi, and align your left foot with your right, so that your back is to the temaeza and you are standing directly facing the sadōguchi. Sit down, and rest the kensui in front of your knees with the hishaku that is resting on the kensui parallel to the sadōguchi threshold (14). Close the fusuma (15).

Pick up the kensui with your left hand, and from your left leg (16), stand up.

Footwork when entering the tea room and immediately turning around to face the sadōguchi

sadōguchi

Turn your right foot inward and step in front of your left foot, bring the heel of your left foot around 180° so that you can face in the opposite direction, and align your right foot with your left, so that you are standing facing the temaeza. From your left foot, proceed toward the temaedatami (17). Sit at your *teiza* (see page 8 about the *teiza*) (18), and set down the kensui (19).

Take the hishaku below the node with your left hand (20) and, while rotating that hand inward, bring the hishaku vertically in front of you. With your right hand, reposition the hishaku so that the cup faces you straight forward. Re-hold the handle with the left thumb and forefinger, and

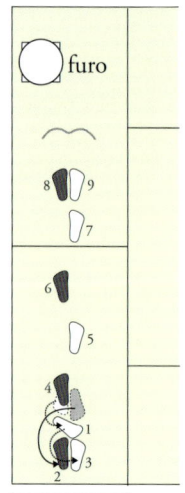

Footwork when proceeding to the temaeza with the kensui

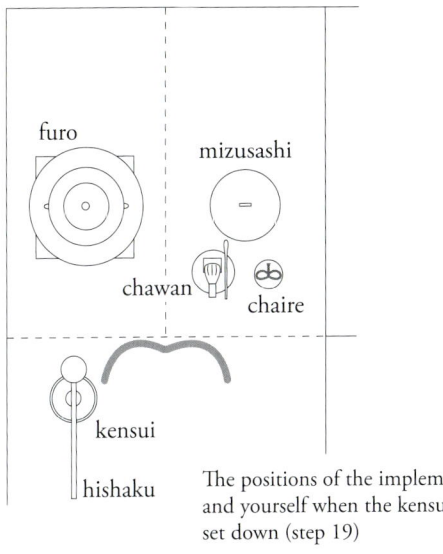

The positions of the implements and yourself when the kensui is set down (step 19)

straighten your right hand fingers, keeping the fingertips just touching the handle end, to take the set posture (*kamae*) called *kagami-bishaku*, the "mirror ladle" pose (21). See "*Kagami-bishaku*," page 52, *Urasenke Tea Procedure Guidebook 1*. Pass your right hand between the ladle handle and yourself and use it to draw the futaoki out of the kensui (22). Bring the futaoki in front of yourself (23), and then around to the front of the hishaku to set it down so that it is centered left-right between the *shikiita* and the tatami bordering on the left and is just outside the imaginary line extending leftward from the front edge of the *shikiita* (24).

Grasp the hishaku handle from the front with your right hand, set the hishaku cup on the futaoki (25), and lay its handle down on the tatami at the natural angle it comes to by pulling your elbow back toward you naturally. Now, for the opening bow between host and guests (*shukyaku sōrei*), make a *sō* bow (26). See "Bowing – the Three Types of Bows," pages 28–29, *Urasenke Tea Procedure Guidebook 1*. [Note: Here, the guests simultaneously make a *shin* bow to the host.]

With your left hand, move the kensui forward so that it is flush with your knee line (27). Make sure your clothing is not in disarray, and pause in the proper sitting position for a moment of concentration (28).

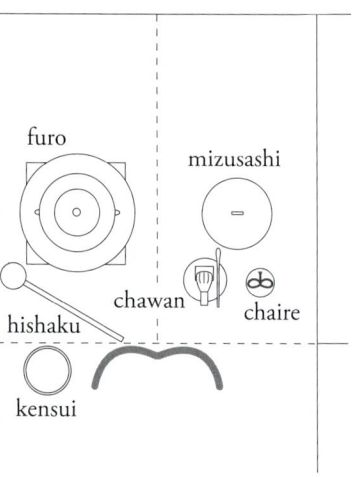

The positions of the implements and yourself when the kensui has been moved forward (step 27)

Removing the chaire from the shifuku

Pick up the chawan from the right-front with your right hand (29), hold it from the left side with your left hand (30), re-hold it from the right side with your right hand, and set it down in front of you (31), leaving enough space between it and your knees to next set the clothed chaire. Pick up the clothed chaire with your right hand (32) and set it down in front of you in the space between the chawan and your knees (33).

Undo the first knot of the shifuku cord using both hands (34, 35). Hold the clothed chaire steady with your left hand as you take hold of the front loop of the shifuku cord with your right forefinger and middle finger on top and thumb underneath (36). Pull the cord toward you (37), and then, to un-twist the cord, rotate your wrist so that your thumb comes above (38).

Grasp the clothed chaire from above with your right hand (39), pick it up slightly, turn it 90° counter-clockwise so that the loose cord is on the right, and set it down (40). Put your right thumb and forefinger at the left-hand side of the shifuku's thread loops (*tsugari*) to hold them in place, and pull the braided-together end of the cord (*uchidome*) with your left hand (41). With the thumb and forefinger of both hands, gently spread the shifuku fabric out along the *tsugari* thread loops, first spreading out the far side (42), then the near side (43).

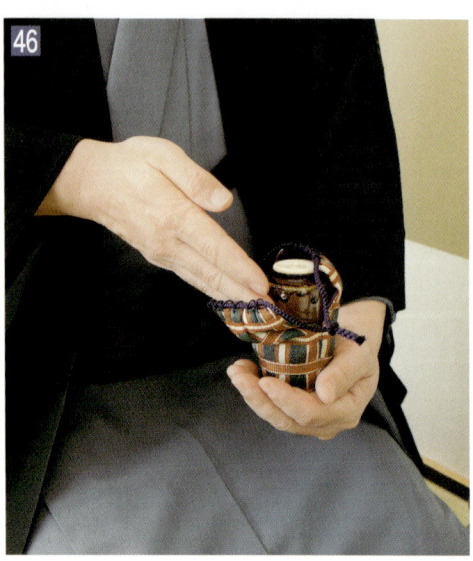

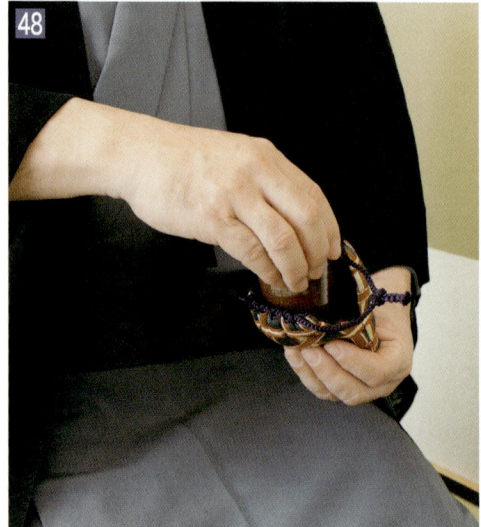

Pick up the clothed chaire from above with your right hand (44), turn it 90° clockwise so that the loose cord faces you once again, and place it in your left palm (45).

Prepare the chaire for removal from the shifuku by sliding your extended fingers between the chaire and shifuku — first on the right side (46), then the left (47). Hold the chaire from above with your right hand, slide the shifuku off with your left hand (48), and set the chaire down in front of you (49). Straighten out the shifuku using both hands (50), take the right side of the shifuku with your right hand, and flip the shifuku over from right to left onto your left palm (51). The braided-together end of the

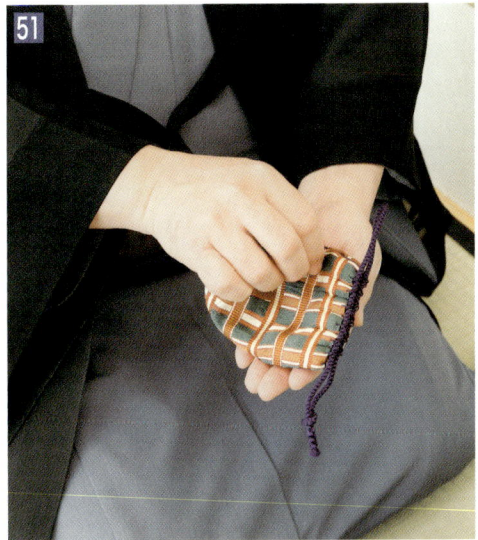

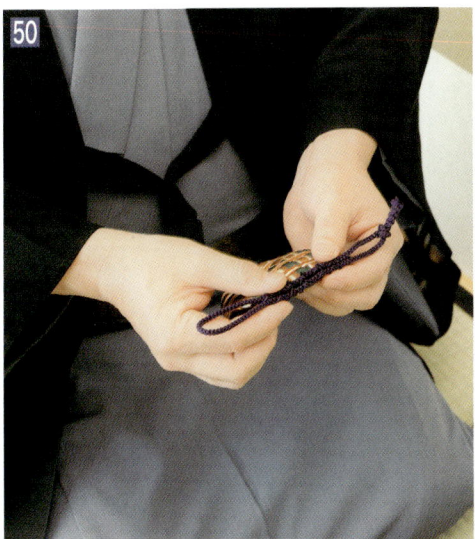

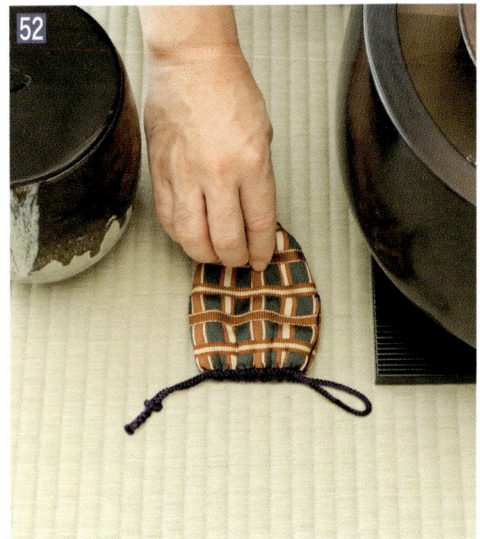

cord should now be on the side closer to the guests. Hold the bottom part of the shifuku with your right hand and place the shifuku left-right centered between the *shikiita* and mizusashi and somewhat past their front-back midpoint (52), but taking care that the top does not extend further than the *shikiita*.

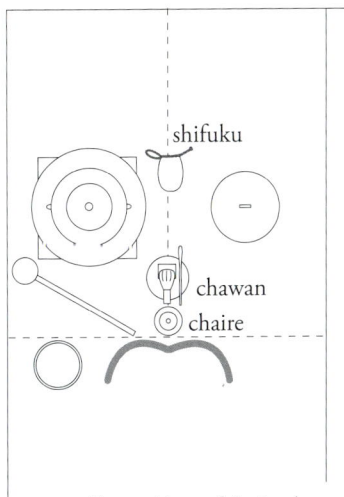

The positions of the implements when the shifuku has been set down (step 52)

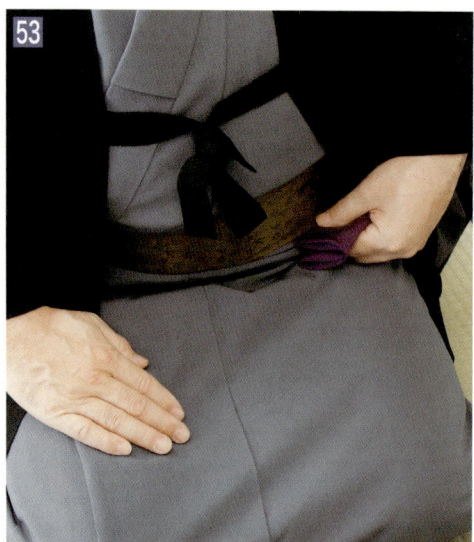

Folding the fukusa in *sō-no-yohōsabaki*

Take your fukusa from your obi with your left hand (53), slide your right forefinger inside the upper right loose corner, and grasp that corner with the right thumb and forefinger (54). Release your left hand, whereby the fukusa becomes totally un-folded. Place your left thumb and fingers next to your right thumb and fingers to loosely clasp the top edge of the fukusa. Maintaining that loose clasp, slide your left hand down to the left-hand corner of the fukusa and hold the fukusa open in front of you. See A illustrations on facing page for the hand movements following step 54.

The following steps will be repeated for all four sides of the fukusa. Grasp the upper right part of the fukusa between the last two fingers and palm of your right hand. You are then free to release the right thumb and first two fingers and bring them next to your left thumb and fingers to grasp the corner held in the left hand. The first time you do this, simultaneously turn your upper body slightly away from the guests. Loosen your left hand grasp, and pull the fukusa through your left hand fingers until they can grasp the next corner, at the same time releasing the part of the fukusa held in your right hand palm. See B illustrations on facing page. Hold the fukusa open again. Focusing your eyes on the upper

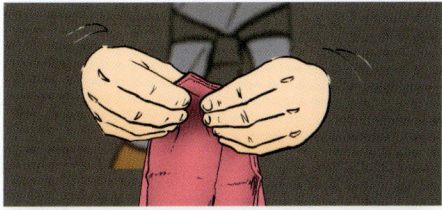

A: How to grasp and hold the fukusa open at the start of *sō-no-yohōsabaki*

B: How to re-grasp the fukusa and advance to the next fukusa side in *sō-no-yohōsabaki*

portion of the fukusa, slowly bring your hands together slightly, loosening your pull on the fukusa for a couple of moments (55). Slowly stretch your hands apart (56). Repeat the B illustration movements and steps 55, 56 for the remaining three sides.

Once you are holding the fukusa open again for the last time (as in step 56), the *wasa* side should be to the right as when you started. Re-hold the corner held in your left hand with the right thumb and first two fingers, but this time maintaining your grasp on the upper right part of the fukusa held in your right palm. Pull the fukusa through your left hand fingers and hold the next corner as before, this time releasing the corner held by your right thumb and first two fingers, and simultaneously returning your upper body to the facing forward position. The fukusa corner has fallen away from you, and the fukusa is in the usual triangle shape. Reestablish your grasp on the corners, thumbs toward you and the fingers outside (57). Fold the fukusa as you would to purify a natsume (58). See "Folding the fukusa," pages 37–39, *Urasenke Tea Procedure Guidebook 1*.

Purifying the chaire and chashaku

Pick up the chaire from the side with your left hand and bring it directly in front of you over your knees. In two straight left to right motions, wipe the lid's far and near surfaces as though writing the Chinese numeral "二" (59). Lightly press the fukusa against the body of the chaire, keep it in place there as you open your hand and let the fukusa open one fold in your palm, and wipe the body by rotating the chaire counter-clockwise using your left fingers (60). After making three full rotations, slide your right hand and the fukusa downwards off the chaire (61).

Lightly rest your right hand, which is loosely clutching the fukusa, on your right thigh as you place the chaire down to the front left of the mizusashi, where the chawan previously was (62).

Refold the fukusa for purifying the chashaku, rest it on your left palm (63), and take the chashaku with your right hand (64). Purify the chashaku in the standard manner (65). See "Purifying the chashaku," pages 44–45, *Urasenke Tea Procedure Guidebook 1*. Place the chashaku on the lid of the chaire so that it is on the left of the lid knob and points straight ahead (66).

Examining the chasen

Take the handle of the chasen with your right thumb and forefinger, and stand the chasen to the right of the chaire, where the chaire previously was (67). If the mizusashi has a lacquered lid, purify the lid as follows: Transfer the folded fukusa to your right hand by placing the right thumb into the folded-over fukusa and right fingers under that right side. Push the left side of the fukusa under to fold the fukusa in half, place your right fingers under the fukusa to hold the half-folded fukusa with your right hand, and "*tenari*" (at the position where the natural movement of the arm and hand do so) wipe the front half of the mizusashi lid as though writing the Chinese numeral "二" (68). Then transfer the fukusa back to your left hand. [Note: If the mizusashi lid is of the same material as the mizusashi, there is no need to purify the lid, so move directly from step 67 to step 69.] Take the chawan with your right hand from the right side and set it slightly closer to yourself (69). Take the chakin from the chawan and place it on the mizusashi lid (70).

At this point, the procedure differs slightly depending on whether or not the use of a fukusa is prescribed for handling the kettle lid. If the use of a fukusa is not prescribed, return the fukusa to your obi

(where it will stay until step 144, page 43). The instructions that follow assume use of the fukusa.

With your right hand, hold the lower fold on the right side of the fukusa, and as the upper fold drops to the left, clasp it between the index finger and middle finger of your left hand (71). Pick up the hishaku with your right hand, grasp the handle just below the node with your left thumb and forefinger, and take the set posture as in step 21, page 13 (72). Hold the fukusa with your right hand, place it on the kettle lid, and utilize it to grasp the knob and remove the lid (73). Rest the lid on the futaoki (74).

Handling the kettle lid

Women employ the fukusa any time they remove the kettle lid from the kettle. Men normally use the fukusa if the lid knob is made of *nanryō* silver or if the lid is of the same material as the kettle (*tomobuta*). In both cases, the knob will be prone to high levels of heat transfer.

Holding the right side of the folded fukusa in your right hand, pass the fukusa between the hishaku handle and yourself and set it down behind the kensui (75).

Hold the end of the hishaku handle with your right hand and bring your right hand around so that the hishaku is horizontal and over your knees, and its cup is facing upward. Hold the handle from underneath and in the position for using the hishaku. Then scoop hot water from the kettle (76) and pour it into the chawan (77). Rest the hishaku on the kettle in the *oki-bishaku* manner (78). See "Oki-bishaku," page 53, *Urasenke Tea Procedure Guidebook 1*.

Take the chasen with your right hand (79) and conduct *chasentōshi*, the examining of the chasen, gently raising it twice to check the tines (80). See "Examining the chasen," pages 46–47, *Urasenke Tea Procedure Guidebook 1*. Slowly remove the chasen from the chawan (81), and return it to where it was.

Take the chawan from the side with your right hand, transfer it to your left hand, and pour the water out into the kensui (82).

Wiping the chawan

Take the chakin from the mizusashi lid with your right hand (83), set it inside the chawan, hold the portion having the puff with your right thumb and forefinger, and drape the portion you are holding over the left edge of the chawan. Wipe the chawan by rotating the chakin around it about three-and-a-half times (84). Pull the chakin off of the chawan, lay it inside the chawan, fold the far portion inward, re-hold the chakin in order to wipe the chawan interior, and swab the interior as if writing the hiragana characters "い" and "り". Set the chakin inside the chawan, re-hold the chawan with your right hand, and set it down in front of you (85). See "How to wipe the chawan," pages 50–51, *Urasenke Tea Procedure Guidebook 1*. Place the chakin on the kettle lid *tenari* (86).

Making and serving the koicha

Take the chashaku with your right hand (87). Take the chaire from the side with your left hand (88) and, as you bring it to the left side of the chawan, adjust your right-hand hold on the chashaku to grasp it deep in your palm with your ring finger and little finger. Holding the chaire tilted at a slight angle so that the mouth is over the chawan (89), use the freed fingers of your right hand to remove its lid and rest the lid to the right of the chawan (90).

Put three heaping scoops of tea into the chawan (91). Rest the chashaku on the right side of the chawan rim pointing straight ahead, and conduct *mawashidashi* (turning the container to get the contents out) of the tea as follows: Support the chaire with your right hand, and rotate the chaire counter-clockwise, tilting it to pour the remaining tea into the chawan (92). With your right thumb and forefinger, wipe the far and near edges of the chaire mouth as though writing the hiragana character "こ" (93), and wipe off those fingers on the kaishi paper tucked in your kimono. Replace the lid of the chaire with your right hand, and return the chaire to its former position beside the chasen with your left hand (94). Take the chashaku with your right hand, and use the tip to spread out the tea within the chawan (95). Give the chashaku a light tap against the rim of the chawan to remove the excess tea (96). Return the chashaku to its former position on top of the chaire (97).

With your right hand, grasp the mizusashi lid handle (98), take the lid off the mizusashi, and bring it in front of you. Hold the left side of the lid with your left hand (99).

Release your right hand, twist your left hand so that the top side of the lid faces to the right, and hold the vertical lid with your right hand at a spot just above where the left hand is holding it. With your right hand, lean the lid against the left side of the mizusashi (100). The mizusashi lid handle should be on the side leaning against the mizusashi.

With your right hand, grasp the hishaku handle from above (101), remove the hishaku from the kettle, grasp the handle at the node with your left hand, adjust your right hand position to hold the hishaku for use, and scoop water from the mizusashi (102). Pour the water into the kettle (103).

[Note: Water is added to the kettle to adjust the hot water temperature only during koicha temae when using a furo.] Then immediately scoop hot water from the kettle (104), pour the desired amount for beginning the blending process into the chawan (105), pour the excess amount back into the kettle, and rest the hishaku on the kettle in the *kiri-bishaku* manner (106, 107). See "Taking the hishaku in order to draw water from the water jar," page 57, and "*Kiri-bishaku*," page 54, *Urasenke Tea Procedure Guidebook 1*.

Take the chasen with your right hand and, as you stabilize the chawan with your left hand, carefully blend the tea and hot water together (108).

Amount of hot water

While there is a fairly wide variation in the consistency of koicha based upon factors such as the number of guests, implements used, preferences, and so on, to each portion of 3.75 g. of the powdered tea, around 30-40 cc of hot water is added over the first and second pourings from the hishaku. In the first pouring (step 105), enough hot water should be poured into the chawan to enable you to make a smooth initial blend. Afterwards (step 110), the additional amount to make the proper consistency is added, and then the final blending is conducted.

Rest the chasen handle against the left side of the chawan rim, and once again take a scoop of hot water from the kettle (109). With your left hand, grasp the chasen and raise it slightly. Add enough hot water to the chawan as needed for the amount of koicha you intend to prepare, by pouring it over the chasen tines (110), and then again rest the chasen handle against the left side of the chawan rim. Pour the excess hot water back into the kettle (111), and rest the hishaku on the kettle in the *oki-bishaku* manner (112).

With your right hand, grasp the chasen and, while stabilizing the chawan with your left hand, continue blending the tea. End slowly in a circular motion as if writing the hiragana character "の", and quietly pull both hands from the chawan (113). Return the chasen to its former place (114). Pick up the chawan with your right hand, place it on your left palm, turn the chawan in two clockwise moves so that the front faces away from you (115), and set the chawan out on the adjacent tatami, at a spot slightly down from your knee line (116, 117). If the chawan is NOT Raku ware, place your kobukusa out next to it, as described on page 36. Once you have placed the chawan (and kobukusa) out, rest your hands slightly apart on your lap, and wait until the first guest takes the first sip of the koicha.

If the chawan is NOT Raku ware, place your kobukusa out next to it. Before entering the tea room in the first place, your kobukusa, in its folded-in-half state, will be tucked inside your kimono so that the folded side (*wasa*) is to the bottom and the kobukusa edge with no seam is at the top of the half that is away from you. The following are the steps for placing it out with the koicha: After setting the chawan out ①, immediately with your right hand take the kobukusa from your kimono by holding the bottom folded edge with your fingers toward you and thumb away from you, and rest it on your left palm so the *wasa* is to the right ②. Release your right hand and re-hold the kobukusa by rotating your wrist and placing your fingers under the opposite side of the kobukusa and thumb on top ③, then set the kobukusa down to the lower side (*geza*) of the chawan, so that the *wasa* is to your left (i.e. the guests' right)④. Rest your hands slightly apart on your lap ⑤, and wait until the first guest takes the first sip of the koicha.

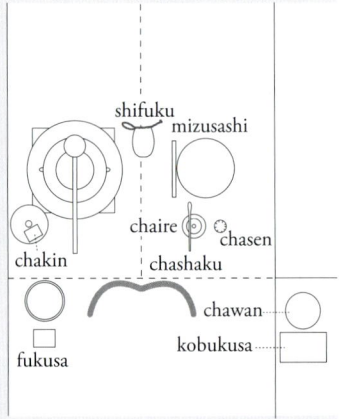

The positions of the implements when the chawan and kobukusa have been set out (⑤)

As described in detail in "Knowledge for Guests: Partaking of Koicha" in this guidebook, once the koicha is ready, the first guest retrieves it (and the kobukusa), the guests bow in unison, and the first guest begins to drink the koicha.

Once the first guest takes the first sip, make a *sō* bow and inquire about the quality of the koicha that you have prepared "Ofukukagen wa?" (118). Then adjust your sitting position to sit diagonally facing the *kyakutsuki* side of the temaeza, the side which is nearer to the guests.

Once the second guest begins to drink the koicha, the first guest inquires about the name of the tea, the producer of the tea, the name and maker of the confection, and related points of interest. Respond to the questions (119).

When the last guest takes the last sip, return to *imae*; that is, to the forward-facing sitting position for conducting the temae (120). Grasp the hishaku handle from above with your right hand (121), and remove the hishaku from the kettle.

Re-hold the hishaku for use, scoop water from the mizusashi, and pour the water into the kettle (122). Rest the hishaku on the kettle in the *hiki-bishaku* manner (123). See "*Hiki-bishaku*," page 55, *Urasenke Tea Procedure Guidebook 1*. After this, pick up the fukusa from the right side with your right hand, place it on your left palm flipped right to left so that the loose corners are on top, take the uppermost triangular corner with your right thumb and forefinger, and let the fukusa fall away from your left hand, so that it hangs from your right hand in the form of a large triangle. In the standard manner, fold that into two (124), and tuck the fukusa into your obi. See "Hanging the fukusa from your obi" steps 4–10, pages 35–36, *Urasenke Tea Procedure Guidebook 1*. Wait for the guests to conduct *haiken* of the chawan (and kobukusa) and for the first guest, together with the last guest, to then return it (them) to where you had originally set it (them) out (125).

If, after step 117, no kobukusa was placed out with the koicha, then when the chawan is returned (126) and the first and last guests have returned to their seats, pick the chawan up with your right hand, rest it on your left palm, re-hold it directly from the side with your right hand, and place it in front of you (127). Here again is a bow between host and guests (*shukyaku sōrei*). Make a *sō* bow (128).

If, after step 117, you set out a kobukusa, then when the chawan and the kobukusa are returned, first take the kobukusa with your right hand from the right side with your thumb on top and fingers below ① and tuck it into the front fold of your kimono ②. Then, pick the chawan up and place it in front of you as described in step 127, after which comes the bow between host and guests (*shukyaku sōrei*)(128).

Lift up the bottom tip of the hishaku handle from underneath with your right hand, slide your hand up the handle to hold the hishaku for use, scoop hot water from the kettle, and pour it into the chawan (129). Rest the hishaku on the kettle in the *oki-bishaku* manner (130).

Take the chawan with your right hand, transfer it to your left hand, and pour the water out into the kensui (131). Return the chawan to its place in front of you with your right hand. Then make a *sō* bow and inform the first guest that you will conclude the temae ("Oshimai itashimasu") [Note: If koicha temae will be followed by usucha temae, say that you will conclude the temae for the moment, "Ichiō oshimai itashimasu"] (132).

Concluding the temae

With your right hand, grasp the hishaku handle from above, remove the hishaku from the kettle, grasp the handle at the node with your left hand, adjust your right hand position to hold the hishaku for use (133), and scoop water from the mizusashi (134). Pour the water into the chawan (135). Rest the hishaku on the kettle in the *hiki-bishaku* manner (136).

Take the chasen with your right hand and conduct the simple version of *chasentōshi*, in which the chasen is only raised once to check the tines (137). Return the chasen to where it was (138). Take the chawan with your right hand, transfer it to your left hand, and pour the water out into the kensui (139). Take the chakin from the kettle lid with your right hand and set it in the chawan (140).

Re-hold the chawan with your right hand and set it down in front of you (141). Take the chasen with your right hand and set it in the chawan, making sure that the knot of the thread at the base of its tines (*kagariito*) is facing upward (142). Take the chashaku with your right hand (143), and, resting that hand lightly on your right thigh, move the kensui back and closer to the wall with your left hand (144).

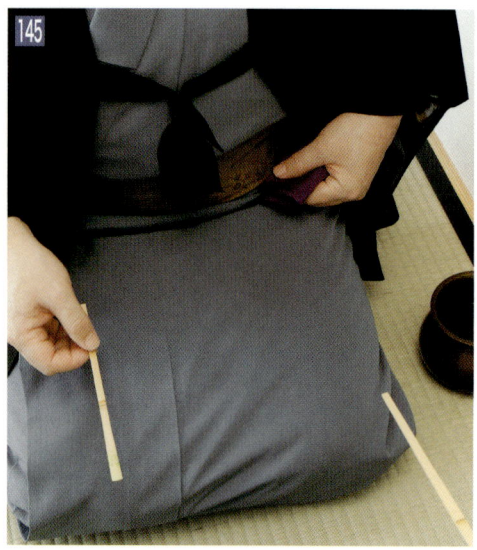

With your left hand, remove your fukusa from your obi (145). Adjust your right-hand hold on the chashaku to grasp it deep in your palm with your ring finger and little finger. Fold the fukusa for purifying the chashaku (146), readjust your right-hand hold on the chashaku, and conduct the simple version of purifying the chashaku, sliding the fukusa down it only twice (147). Place the chashaku on the chawan, scoop facing downward (148). Keep the fukusa held folded inside your left hand and rest that hand lightly on your left thigh. Hold the chawan from the side with your right hand, and move it somewhat leftward from center (149). Then pick up the chaire with your right hand and set it to the right of the chawan (150), so that it and the chawan evenly straddle the imaginary left-right center line of the temaeza. This represents the "midpoint closure" style of implement positioning, called *nakajimai*. Dust off the fukusa over the kensui (151), and return the fukusa to your obi.

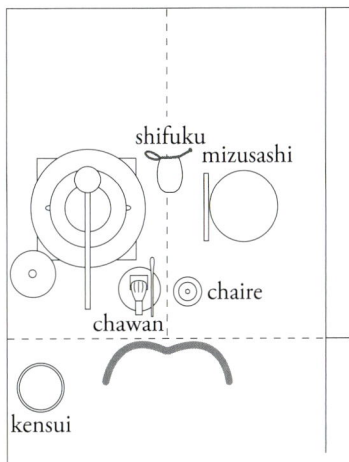

The positions of the implements when the chawan and chaire have been placed at *nakajimai* (step 150)

If the room is a *koma* (small room no more than 4.5 tatami in floor space), the rule after step 148 is to conduct the "conventional closure" style of implement positioning, *honjimai*, and not *nakajimai*. For this, after step 148, dust off the fukusa over the kensui and return it to your obi. Then take the chaire with your right hand and place it to the front right of the mizusashi, as placed in step 9, page 10. Pick up the chawan from the side with your right hand, hold it from the left side with your left hand, re-hold it from the right-front with your right hand, and place it to the front left of the mizusashi, as placed in step 12.

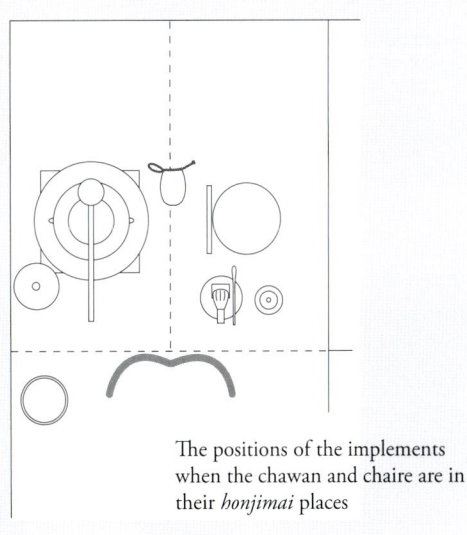

The positions of the implements when the chawan and chaire are in their *honjimai* places

Employ the *tori-bishaku* technique to take the hishaku from the kettle and re-hold it for use (152). Scoop a ladleful of water from the mizusashi, and pour it into the kettle (153). Grasp the hishaku handle just below the node with your left thumb and forefinger, take the set posture with the hishaku, and while your left hand holds the hishaku steady, replace the lid onto the kettle with your right hand, setting it slightly ajar as it was at the start (154). Grasp the hishaku handle from the front with your right hand, and rest the hishaku on the futaoki (155).

Grasp the mizusashi lid with your right hand (156), and bring it in front of yourself. In the reverse of when you removed the lid from the mizusashi, hold the vertical lid with your left hand at a spot just below where the right hand is holding it, and as you twist your left hand to make the lid horizontal, grasp the handle with your right hand (157) and replace the lid onto the mizusashi (158).

Setting out the implements for *haiken*

At the point when you close the mizusashi lid, the first guest asks to do *haiken* of the chaire, chashaku, and shifuku. Acknowledge that request with a *sō* bow (159). [Note: Guests for koicha as a general rule always ask for *haiken*.]

Pick up the hishaku with your right hand (160).

Transfer the hishaku to your left hand, and set it on the kensui facing downward and with the cup hanging outside the rim (161). Take the futaoki with your right hand (162), transfer it to your left hand (163), and set it down behind the kensui (164). Pick up the chawan from the right-front with your right hand (165) and directly place it on the *kattetsuki* side of the temaeza (166). [Note: If you conducted the "conventional closure"(*honjimai*) style of implement positioning, at step 165 you pick up the chawan from the right-front with your right hand, hold it from the left side with your left hand, re-hold it from the right side with your right hand, and then place it on the *kattetsuki* side of the temaeza.]

Pick up the chaire from the side with your right hand (167), place it in your left palm, and adjust your sitting position to sit diagonally facing the *kyakutsuki* side of the temaeza (168). Set the chaire down in front of you with your right hand (169). Take the fukusa from your obi and fold it in the standard way, as though you are about to purify a natsume (170).

Pick up the chaire from the side with your left hand (171). As in steps 59–60, wipe the lid's far and near surfaces as though writing the Chinese numeral "二", press the fukusa against the body of the chaire and let the fukusa open one fold in your palm, and wipe the body by rotating the chaire counter-clockwise using your left fingers (172). After making two full rotations, slide your right hand and the fukusa downwards off the chaire, and set the fukusa down in front of you (173). Remove the chaire lid with your right hand, glance at the underside of the lid (174), then set the lid down on the far side of the fukusa (175).

Immediately pick up the fukusa with

your right hand, lightly press its top side against the body of the chaire, and re-grasp the fukusa so that it is folded back into its fully folded state (176). Wipe the far and near edges of the mouth of the chaire (177). Set the fukusa on the tatami where it was a moment ago (178), immediately pick up the chaire lid, and replace it on the chaire.

With your right hand, hold the chaire from the right side, place it on your left palm, turn it in two clockwise moves so that the front faces away from you (179), and set it in the corner of the adjacent tatami, at a point approximately one medium-sized natsume away from the tatami bordering in both directions (180).

52　*Furo Koicha Temae*

Return the fukusa to your obi, and return to the *imae* sitting position. Pick up the chashaku with your right hand (181), turn it so that the scoop faces upward as you transfer it to your left hand (182), and again adjust your sitting position to diagonally face *kyakutsuki* (183). Re-hold the chashaku from above just below the node with your right thumb and forefinger so that the thumb comes to the right of the chashaku and the fingers are to its left, and set the chashaku down on the lower side (*geza*) of the chaire, its handle pointing toward the guests (184). See detailed images of the chashaku handling in *Urasenke Tea Procedure Guidebook 2*, page 41.

    Return again to *imae* (185), take the shifuku with your right hand (186), and rest it on your left palm (187). Once again adjust your sitting position to diagonally face *kyakutsuki* (188). Place your right thumb on top of the base of the shifuku and fingers on the base, and set the shifuku on the *geza* side of the chashaku with its base toward the guests (189, 190).

How to re-hold the shifuku to place it out with the base toward the guests
(steps 189, 190)

Removing the tea implements

Return to the *imae* sitting position (191). Pick up the hishaku with your left hand, bring it in front of you, and redirect its handle with your right hand so that the hishaku is horizontal and its cup is to the left and facing upward. Clench your right hand fingers around the hishaku handle at the node and hold the hishaku steady in that position as you pick up the futaoki from the side with your left hand and grasp it from the top with your right thumb, forefinger, and middle finger (192). Adjust your sitting position about one knee's-breadth toward the *kattetsuki* side of the temaeza (193), pick up the kensui with your left hand, and stand up leading with your left leg (194). Turn away from the guests, proceed to the sadōguchi, making all the tatami-to-tatami cross-overs with your left foot, and sit facing the closed sadōguchi.

Set the kensui down in front of your knees (195). Take the futaoki with your left hand and set it down to the right of the kensui (196). Hold the hishaku handle from underneath with your left thumb and first two fingers, then re-grasp the handle with your right hand so that you can turn the hishaku cup downward. Rest the hishaku on the kensui so that it is parallel with the sadōguchi threshold and its downward-facing cup is

hanging to the left outside the kensui rim (197). Open the sadōguchi fusuma (198). Then, in the reverse process of the manner in which you set the kensui, futaoki, and hishaku down, hold them as you were holding them before, stand from your left leg, step up to the threshold with your right foot, and cross into the mizuya with your left foot.

Once the host goes to the mizuya with the kensui, the first guest goes to get the chaire, chashaku, and shifuku, and brings them back to his seat. See "*Haiken* of the Chaire, Chashaku, and Shifuku" steps 2–6, pages 139–141 herein.

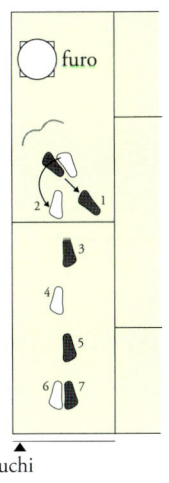

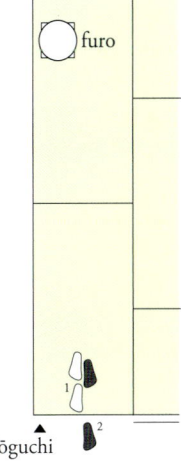

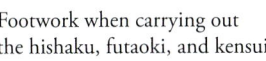

Footwork when carrying out the hishaku, futaoki, and kensui

Footwork when leaving the room after opening the fusuma

Having set aside the kensui, futaoki, and hishaku in the mizuya, return to the temaeza and sit at the *imae* position. Pick up the chawan with your right hand, place it in your left palm, and steady it with your right hand. Stand up, leading with your left foot (199). This time, move your left foot diagonally back to the left and then bring your right foot to the lower end of the temaedatami so as to turn toward the guests, and take the chawan to the mizuya (200). Again return to the temaeza, but, this time, adjust your path to the right half of the temaedatami in order to sit down in front of the mizusashi. Hold the mizusashi deeply with both hands (201), stand up, turn toward the guests as before, and take the mizusashi to the mizuya (202). Upon exiting, turn around to face the sadōguchi, sit down, set the mizusashi down in front of your knees (203), and close the fusuma (204).

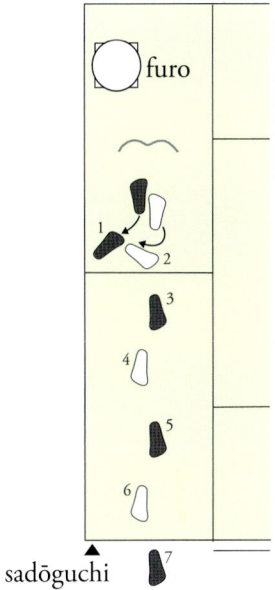

Footwork when taking the chawan to the mizuya

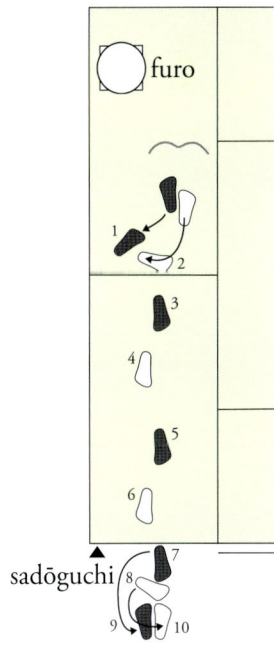

Footwork when taking the mizusashi to the mizuya and sitting to close the sadōguchi fusuma

Once the host closes the fusuma, the first guest does *tsugirei* to the next guest and starts the *haiken*. When all the guests in turn have finished their *haiken*, the last guest takes the items to the first guest, who comes forward to a spot near where the host set them out and there gets them from the last guest. The first guest then sets them back on the tatami adjacent to the temaedatami. (This procedure in which the first and last guests meet in order to return the items to the host is called *deai de kaesu*.) See "*Haiken* of the Chaire, Chashaku, and Shifuku" steps 7–18, pages 140–144 herein.

Retrieving the *haiken* items

Sit at the sadōguchi. When it seems that the *haiken* items have been returned, open the fusuma and, once you have confirmed that the guests are settled back in their seats, stand from your right leg and proceed to the temaedatami, making all the tatami-to-tatami cross-overs with your right foot. Sit so that the *haiken* items are directly in front of you. The first guest thanks you with a bow. Return that bow (205). Then answer any questions about the items (206).

Take the shifuku from the base with your right hand (207). Place it on your left palm. Take the chashaku with your right hand (208). Rest it at an angle on top of the shifuku, and lightly hold it in place with your left thumb (209). Take the chaire from the side with your right hand (210).

Holding the chaire and chashaku/shifuku in front of you, stand up leading with your left leg, then bring your right foot to the lower end of the temaedatami and return to the mizuya, making all the tatami-to-tatami cross-overs with your left foot (211). Upon entering the mizuya, turn around to face the sadōguchi, and sit down (212).

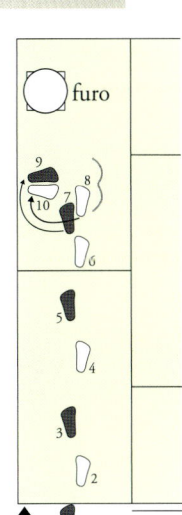

Footwork when coming in and sitting to retrieve the *haiken* items

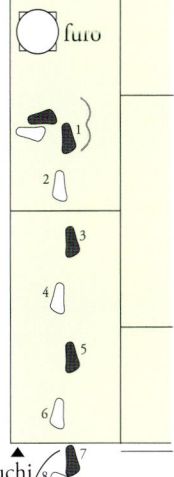

Footwork when exiting with the *haiken* items and turning to sit at the sadōguchi for the final bow

59

Set the chaire down close to your knee on the side toward the wall post (*tatetsuke*). Take the chashaku with your right hand and set it next to the chaire on the side toward the wall post. IF the wall post is on your left, then take the shifuku from the base with your right hand, and set it next to the chashaku (213). [IF the wall post is on your right, the shifuku must be flipped over before you set it next to the chashaku. See Ro Koicha Temae steps 238–239, page 122 herein.] Make a formal *shin* bow (214), and close the fusuma.

Setting the shifuku down with the chaire and chashaku

Whenever the chaire, chashaku, and shifuku are set down together, the braided-together end (*uchidome*) of the shifuku cord must be on the side of the shifuku that is closer to the chaire. It may therefore be necessary to flip the shifuku over before setting it down. This will not be necessary for the host to do at the end of a koicha temae if it is a conventional tea room and the orientation of the sadōguchi in relation to the temaeza is straight forward (*shōmen/tsukkomi sadōguchi*). If, however, it is a conventional tea room and the sadōguchi is at a side position (*mawari/magari sadōguchi*), it will be necessary, because the wall post will be on the host's right at this time.

Ro Koicha Temae

The Preparations

Just as in the furo season, the usual practice in the case of a spacious tea room (*hiroma*) is to place a *furosakibyōbu* in the *kattetsuki* corner at the far end of the temaedatami, to demarcate the implement mat (*dōgudatami*). The ro should have moist ash (*shimeshibai*) sprinkled over the dry ash, the ro charcoal should be in it and heating the kettle which is resting on the trivet, and the lid of the kettle should be ajar. For information about the ro, preparing the ash in it, and positioning the kettle on the trivet, see *Urasenke Tea Procedure Guidebook 2*, pages 52–53.

In the mizuya, preparations are the same as in the furo season. Fill the mizusashi with water to about 80%, and place it at the right-left center of the temaedatami, about 16 tatami weaves, or approximately 24 cm, up from the imaginary line extending from the inner side of the front bordering of the adjacent *kinindatami*. Put enough powdered tea into the chaire for the number of guests, figuring on three heaping chashaku scoops, or 3.75 grams, per person. Then place the chaire inside its shifuku and tie the cord. See "How to tie the shifuku cord" diagrams, page 6 herein. Place the so-readied chaire in front of the mizusashi on the temaedatami.

Have the chawan (set up with the chakin and chasen in it and chashaku resting face down across the right) and kensui (set up with the futaoki in it and ro-use hishaku face down across the top with its cup resting on the rim) ready in the mizuya. Remember to hang your fukusa from your obi and put your sensu aside.

The following temae is presented in an 8-tatami *hiroma* with ro layout in the standard *yojōhangiri* position and sadōguchi in the wall that runs alongside the temaedatami, meaning that the host must change direction upon entry or before being able to exit back into the mizuya. A sadōguchi in this position is referred to as a *mawari-* or *magari-sadōguchi* (roundabout host's doorway).

Carrying out the tea implements

Sit at the closed sadōguchi so that your knees are approximately 16 tatami weaves, or 24 cm, from the threshold, and place the chawan in front of your knees. Open the fusuma (1) Pick up the chawan with your right hand (2), place it in your left palm, and steady it with your right hand (3). Bring your right foot forward slightly, and stand up. To enter, cross the threshold with your right foot (4), and, making the tatami-to-tatami cross-overs with your right foot (5), proceed to the temaeza.

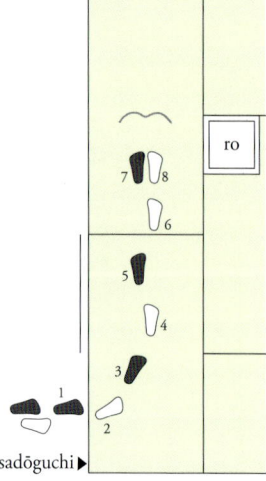

Footwork when entering with the chawan

Sit in front of the mizusashi so that your knees are aligned with the upper side of the ro frame (6).

Grasp the chawan from the right side with your right hand (7), hold it from the left-front with your left hand, and set it down on the *kattetsuki* side of the temaeza (8).

Pick up the chaire with your right hand, and move it to the front right of the mizusashi (9). Pick up the chawan from the left-front with your left hand (10), hold it from the right side with your right hand (11), re-hold it from the side with your left hand (12), and place it to the front left of the mizusashi (13).

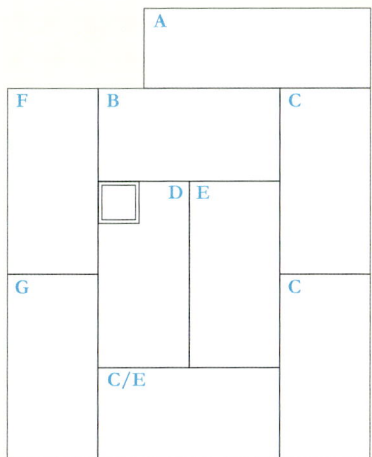

A Alcove / *Tokonoma*
  (Alcove mat / *Tokodatami*)
B High ranking personage's seating / *Kinindatami*
C Guests' seating / *Kyakudatami*
D Ro mat / *Rodatami*
E Traversing mat / *Kayoidatami*
F Temae mat / *Temaedatami*
  (Implement mat / *Dōgudatami*)
G Host's entry mat / *Fumikomidatami*

The functional names of the tatami mats in a standard 8-tatami *hiroma* with ro

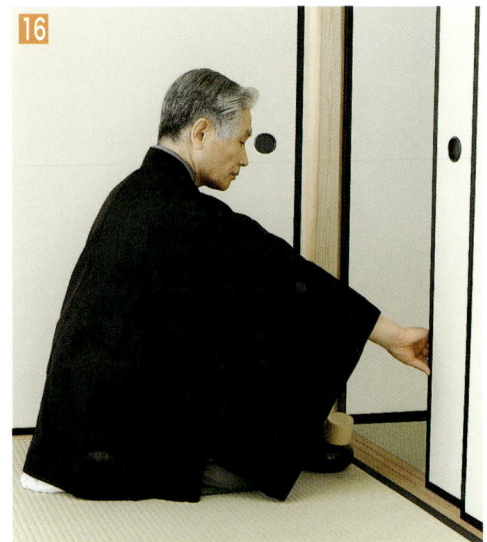

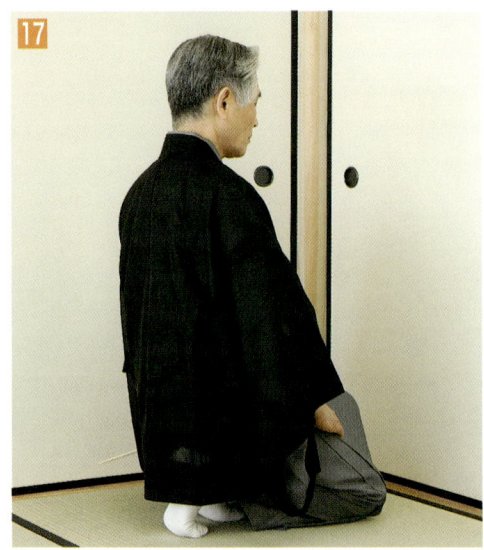

Bring your left foot forward slightly (14), stand, turn in the direction of the guests, and return to the mizuya, making all the tatami-to-tatami cross-overs with your left foot.

Holding the prepared kensui with your left hand, step into the tea room with your right foot (15). Take one step forward with your left foot, turn your right foot inward and step in front of your left foot, bring the heel of your left foot around to the far side of that entry tatami (*fumikomidatami*), and align your right foot with your left, so that you are standing directly facing the sadōguchi. Sit down, and rest the kensui in front of your knees, with the hishaku that is resting on the kensui parallel to the sadōguchi threshold. Close the fusuma (16).

Pick up the kensui with your left hand, and from your left leg (17), stand up. Bring the heel of your left foot around 90° so that it is at the middle of the width of that tatami, and align your right foot with your left, so that you are standing directly facing the temaeza. From your left foot, proceed toward the temaedatami, making the tatami-to-tatami cross-overs with your right foot (18). Once into the temaedatami, take two more small steps, bring your left foot and then right foot around, so that you are standing with body directed at the inner corner (*uchizumi*) of the ro frame joint that is nearest the *dōgudatami*, sit down so that the

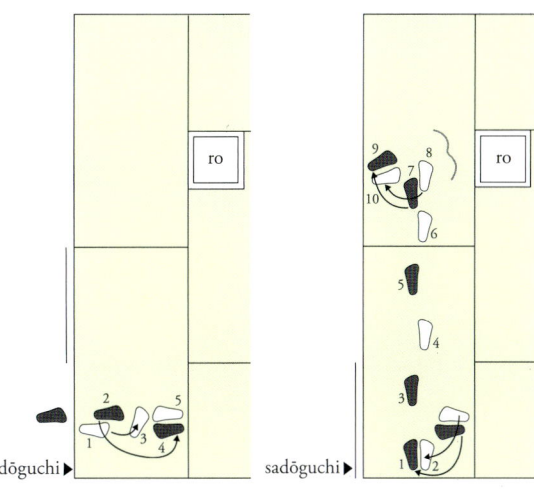

Footwork when entering the tea room and immediately turning around to face the sadōguchi

Footwork when approaching the temaeza with the kensui

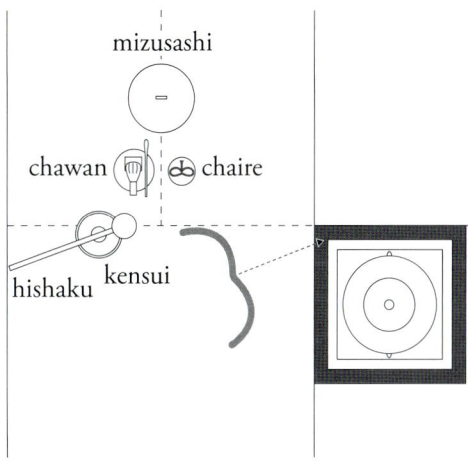

The positions of the implements and yourself when the kensui is set down (step 19)

center of your body is directed at that inner corner and your left knee is along the invisible line that bisects the temaedatami, and set down the kensui (19). Make sure, in taking this seating position, which is the *imae* position for this temae, that there is ample room before your knees to conduct the temae.

If the room is a *koma* (small room no more than 4.5 tatami in floor space), the rule concerning the sitting position to conduct a ro temae is to direct your body at the ro frame's outer corner (*sotozumi*).

Take the hishaku below the node with your left hand (20) and, while rotating that hand inward, bring the hishaku vertically in front of you. With your right hand, re-position the hishaku so that the cup faces you straight forward. Take the set *kagami-bishaku* posture with the hishaku (21). See "*Kagami-bishaku*," page 52, Urasenke Tea Procedure Guidebook 1.

Pass your right hand between the ladle handle and yourself and use it to draw the futaoki out of the kensui (22). Bring the futaoki in front of yourself, and then set it down on the ro tatami so that it is 3 tatami weaves, or about 4.5 cm, away from the tatami bordering and ro frame (23).

Grasp the hishaku handle from the front with your right hand, set the hishaku cup on the futaoki (24), and lay its handle down on the tatami so the hishaku is parallel with your body. Now, for the opening bow between host and guests (*shukyaku sōrei*), make a *sō* bow (25). [Note: Here, the guests simultaneously make a *shin* bow to the host.]

Following this, with your left hand, re-position the kensui so that it is approximately 5–7 tatami weaves, or approximately 7.5–10.5 cm, away from the temaedatami bordering that is on the *kattetsuki* side of the temaedatami and the center of the kensui rests on the imaginary line extending across the temaedatami from the upper side of the ro frame (26). Make sure your clothing is

not in disarray, and pause in the proper sitting position for a moment of concentration (27).

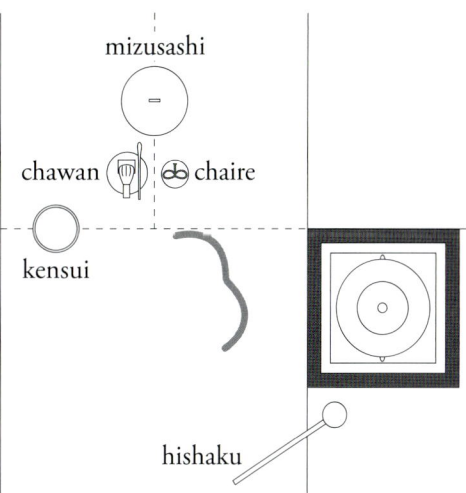

The positions of the implements when the kensui has been re-positioned (step 26)

Removing the chaire from the shifuku

Pick up the chawan from the left side with your left hand (28), re-hold it from the right side with your right hand (29), and set it down in front of you (30), leaving enough space between it and your knees to next set the clothed chaire. Pick up the clothed chaire with your right hand (31) and set it down in front of you in the space between the chawan and your knees (32).

Undo the first knot of the shifuku cord using both hands (33). Hold the clothed chaire steady with your left hand as you take hold of the front loop of the shifuku cord with your right forefinger and middle fingers on top and thumb underneath. Pull the cord toward you (34), and then, to un-twist the cord, rotate your wrist so that your thumb comes above.

Grasp the clothed chaire from above with your right hand, pick it up slightly, turn it 90° counter-clockwise so that the loose cord is on the right, and set it down. Put your right thumb and forefinger at the left-hand side of the shifuku's thread loops (*tsugari*) to hold them in place, and pull out the braided-together end of the cord (*uchidome*) with your left hand. With the thumb and forefinger of both hands, gently spread the shifuku fabric out along the *tsugari* thread loops, first spreading out the far side, then the near side (35).

Pick up the clothed chaire from above with your right hand, turn it 90° clockwise so that the loose cord faces you once again, and place it in your left palm (36). Prepare the chaire for removal from the shifuku by sliding your extended fingers between the chaire and shifuku — first on the right side, then the left (37). Slide the shifuku off the chaire with your left hand as you set the chaire down in front of you with your right hand (38). For close-up photos of the process described in steps 28–38 to remove the shifuku from the chaire, see Furo Koicha photos 35–50, pages 16–19 herein. Straighten out the shifuku using both hands, take the left side of the shifuku with your left hand, and flip the shifuku over from left to right onto your right palm (39). The braided-together end of the cord should now be on the side closer to the guests.

Hold the bottom part of the shifuku with your left hand (40), and place the shifuku centered between the mizusashi and the wall on the *kattetsuki* side of the temaedatami (41).

Folding the fukusa in *sō-no-yohōsabaki*

Regardless of whether it is a furo koicha temae or ro koicha temae, the manner in which to do *sō-no-yohōsabaki* is no different. See "Folding the fukusa in *sō-no-yohōsabaki*," pages 20–21 herein for detailed explanation and illustrations.

Start by taking your fukusa from your obi with your left hand (42). Slide your right forefinger inside the upper right loose corner (43), and grasp that corner.

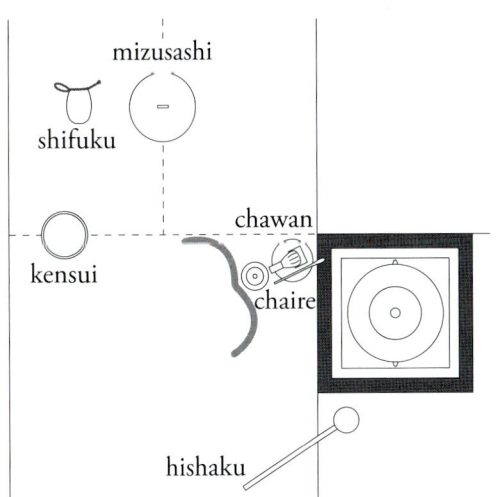

The positions of the implements when the shifuku has been set down (step 41)

Release your left hand, then place your left thumb and fingers next to your right thumb and fingers. Loosely clasping the top edge of the fukusa between the left thumb and fingers, slide your left hand down to the left-hand corner of the fukusa and hold the fukusa open in front of you.

Grasp the upper right part of the fukusa between the last two fingers and palm of your right hand. Bring the right thumb and first two fingers next to your left thumb and fingers to grasp the corner held in the left hand, simultaneously turning your upper body slightly away from the guests. Pull the fukusa through your left hand fingers until they can grasp the next corner, while also releasing the part of the fukusa held in your right hand palm. Hold the fukusa open, now positioned over your left knee (44). Slowly bring your hands together slightly, loosening your pull on the fukusa (45). Slowly stretch your hands apart. Other than the turning of your upper body slightly away from the guests the first time, repeat the steps explained in this paragraph for the remaining three sides.

Once you are holding the fukusa open after the fourth repetition, re-hold the corner held in your left hand with the right thumb and first two fingers. Pull the fukusa through your left hand fingers and hold the next corner as before, but this time release the corner held by your right thumb and first two fingers instead of the corner held in your right palm. At this time, return your upper body to the facing forward position.

Reestablish your grasp on the corners. Fold the fukusa as you would to purify a natsume (46). See "Folding the fukusa," pages 37–39, *Urasenke Tea Procedure Guidebook 1*.

Purifying the chaire and chashaku

Pick up the chaire from the side with your left hand (47) and bring it directly in front of you over your knees. In two straight left to right motions, wipe the lid's far and near surfaces as though writing the Chinese numeral "二" (48). Lightly press the fukusa against the body of the chaire, keep it in place there as you open your hand and let the fukusa open one fold in your palm, and wipe the body by rotating the chaire counter-clockwise using your left fingers (49). After making three full rotations, slide your right hand and the fukusa downward off the chaire.

Lightly rest your right hand, which is loosely clutching the fukusa, on your right thigh as you place the chaire down so that its center rests on the imaginary line extending from the corner of the ro to the center of the mizusashi and the chaire is slightly left of center on that imaginary line (50).

Refold the fukusa for purifying the chashaku, rest it on your left palm, and take the chashaku with your right hand. Purify the chashaku in the standard manner (51). See "Purifying the chashaku," pages 44–45, *Urasenke Tea Procedure Guidebook 1*. Place the chashaku on the lid of the chaire so that it is on the right of the lid knob and it points in an angle that is perpendicular to the imaginary line on which the chaire rests (52).

Examining the chasen

Take the handle of the chasen with your right thumb and forefinger (53), and stand the chasen to the right of the chaire, slightly right of center on that imaginary line from ro corner to mizusashi center (54). If the mizusashi has a lacquered lid, purify the lid as follows: Transfer the folded fukusa to your right hand by placing your right thumb into the folded-over fukusa and right fingers under that right side. Push the left side of the fukusa under to fold the fukusa in half (55), place your right fingers under the fukusa to hold the half-folded fukusa with your right hand, and *tenari* (at the position where the

natural movement of the arm and hand do so) wipe the front half of the mizusashi lid as though writing the Chinese numeral "二" (56). Then transfer the fukusa back to your left hand. [Note: If the mizusashi lid is of the same material as the mizusashi, there is no need to purify the lid, so move directly from step 54 to step 57.] Take the chawan with your right hand from the right side and set it slightly closer to yourself (57).

Take the chakin from the chawan and place it on the mizusashi lid (58).

At this point, the procedure differs slightly depending on whether or not the use of a fukusa is prescribed for handling the kettle lid. See "Handling the kettle lid," page 25 herein. If, as in this example, use of the fukusa is not prescribed, now return it to your obi (where it will stay until step 157) (59). [If use of a fukusa is prescribed, the steps you (hereafter, "Fukusa user:" for your special instructions) are to take now are the same as described for Furo Koicha steps 71–74, page 25 herein. Then temporarily set the fukusa down to your right side beyond your knee line.]

Pick up the end of the hishaku handle with your right hand (60), grasp the handle just below the node with your left thumb and forefinger, take the set posture as in step 21, remove the lid from the kettle, and rest the lid on the futaoki (61). Re-hold the hishaku for use (62), scoop hot water from the kettle (63), and pour it into the chawan (64). Again grasp the hishaku handle just below the node with your left thumb and forefinger, and take the set posture (65). With your right hand, take the kettle lid and put it back on the kettle so that the kettle is completely closed (66). This mid-temae closure of the lid is referred to as *nakabuta*, and is specific to ro koicha temae. [Fukusa user: After step 65, pick up the fukusa with your right hand, utilize it to close the kettle lid, and then return it to its temporary placement spot to

your right side beyond your knee line.]

Grasp the hishaku handle from the front with your right hand, placing your thumb on the left and forefinger on the right, and rest the hishaku on the futaoki in the standard manner for ro temae, setting its cup on the futaoki and laying its handle down on the tatami so the hishaku is parallel with your body (67).

Take the chasen with your right hand (68) and conduct *chasentōshi*, the examining of the chasen (69), raising it twice to check the tines. See "Examining the chasen," pages 46–47, *Urasenke Tea Procedure Guidebook 1*. Return the chasen to where it was (70).

Take the chawan from the side with your right hand (71), transfer it to your left hand, and pour the water out into the kensui (72).

Wiping the chawan

Take the chakin from the mizusashi lid with your right hand (73), and wipe the chawan with it in the standard manner (74). See "How to wipe the chawan," pages 50–51, *Urasenke Tea Procedure Guidebook 1*. Set the chakin inside the chawan, re-hold the chawan with your right hand, and set it down in front of you (75). Return the chakin to the mizusashi lid (76).

Making and serving the koicha

Take the chashaku with your right hand (77). Take the chaire from the side with your left hand (78) and, as you bring it to the left side of the chawan, adjust your right-hand hold on the chashaku to grasp it deep in your palm with your ring finger and little finger. Holding the chaire tilted at a slight angle so that the mouth is over the chawan, use the freed fingers of your right hand to remove its lid (79). Rest the lid to the right of the chawan (80). Put three heaping scoops of tea into the chawan (81). Rest the chashaku on the right side of the chawan rim pointing straight ahead (82), and conduct *mawashidashi* (turning the container to get the contents out) of the tea as follows: Support the chaire with your right hand, and rotate the chaire counter-clockwise, tilting it to pour the remaining tea into the chawan (83). With your right thumb and forefinger, wipe the far and near edges of the chaire mouth as though writing the hiragana character "こ" (84), and wipe off those fingers on the kaishi paper tucked in your kimono. Replace the lid of the chaire with your right hand (85), and return the chaire to its former position beside the chasen with your left hand (86).

Take the chashaku with your right hand, and use the tip to spread out the tea within the chawan (87). Give the chashaku a light tap against the rim of the chawan to remove the excess tea (88). Return the chashaku to its former position on top of the chaire (89).

Pick up the hishaku with your right hand (90), take the set posture with it, and then open the kettle lid with your right hand (91) and rest it on the futaoki (92). [Fukusa user: After step 90 and taking the set posture with the hishaku, pick up the fukusa with your right hand, utilize it to open the kettle lid and rest it on the futaoki, and finally set the fukusa down beside your left knee.] Re-hold the hishaku for use, scoop hot water from the kettle (93), and pour the desired amount for beginning the blending process into the chawan (94). See "Amount of hot water," page 33 herein.

Pour the excess amount back into the kettle (95), and rest the hishaku on the kettle in the standard manner for a ro temae (96); that is, hang the face-down cup just within the mouth of the kettle, and, clasping the handle between your forefinger and middle finger, lower the handle end onto the tatami so that the handle is parallel to the angle at which you are sitting. See "Hishaku use with ro temae," page 58, *Urasenke Tea Procedure Guidebook 1*.

Take the chasen with your right hand (97) and, as you stabilize the chawan with your left hand, carefully blend the tea and hot water together (98).

Rest the chasen handle against the left side of the chawan rim (99). Once again take a scoop of hot water from the kettle.

With your left hand, grasp the chasen and raise it slightly. Add enough hot water to the chawan as needed for the amount of koicha you intend to prepare, by pouring it over the chasen tines (100). Then again rest the chasen handle against the left side of the chawan rim. Pour the excess hot water back into the kettle (101), and rest the hishaku on the kettle in the standard manner.

With your right hand, grasp the chasen and, while stabilizing the chawan with your left hand, continue blending the tea (102).

End slowly in a circular motion as if writing the hiragana character "の", quietly pull both hands from the chawan, and return the chasen to its former place (103).

Pick up the chawan with your right hand (104), place it on your left palm (105), turn the chawan in two clockwise moves so that the front faces away from you (106), and set the chawan out on the adjacent tatami, at a spot slightly down from the kettle lid resting on the futaoki (107, 108). Rest your hands slightly apart on your lap, and wait until the first guest takes the first sip of koicha.

If the chawan is NOT Raku ware, place your kobukusa out next to it as follows: After setting the chawan out (step 107), immediately with your right hand take the kobukusa from your kimono by holding the bottom folded edge (*wasa*) with your fingers toward you and thumb away from you, and rest it on your left palm so that the *wasa* is to the right ①. Release your right hand and re-hold the kobukusa by rotating your wrist and placing your fingers under the opposite side of the kobukusa and thumb on top ②, and then set the kobukusa down to the lower side (*geza*) of the chawan, so that the *wasa* is to your left (i.e. the guests' right) ③.

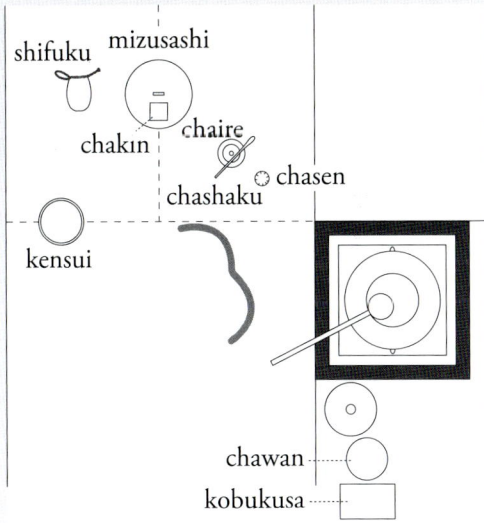

The positions of the implements when the chawan and kobukusa have been set out (③)

Doing *nakajimai*

As described in detail in "Knowledge for Guests: Partaking of Koicha" in this guidebook, once the koicha is ready, the first guest retrieves it (and the kobukusa), the guests bow in unison, and the first guest begins to drink the koicha.

Once the first guest takes the first sip, make a *sō* bow and inquire about the quality of the koicha that you have prepared ("Ofukukagen wa?") (109).

Do *nakajimai*, the "midpoint closure" of the temae which is unique to Ro Koicha temae, as follows: Pick up the hishaku in the standard manner, by grasping the handle from above with your right thumb and forefinger at a point somewhat lower than the node (110), remove the hishaku from the kettle and rotate your hand inward to turn the hishaku cup upward as you bring the hishaku vertically in front of you, re-hold the handle with your left hand, bring your right hand to the bottom of the handle, and take the set posture for a moment. Then, with your right hand, replace the lid onto the kettle, setting it slightly ajar as it was at the start (111). Transfer the hishaku to your left hand and rest it on the kensui so that its cup is facing down and hangs over the kensui and its handle is parallel to your body (112). Take the futaoki with your right hand

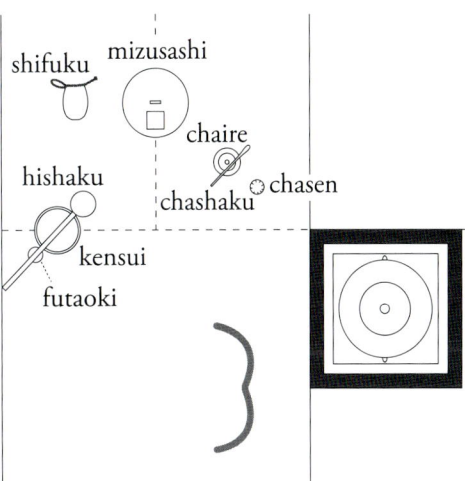

The *nakajimai* position of the implements and yourself (step 115)

(113), set it in your left palm, re-hold it from above with your right hand, re-hold it from the side with your left hand, and set it down behind the kensui under the hishaku handle (114). Shift your sitting position so as to directly face the *kyakutsuki* side of your temaeza and your body is intersected by the invisible line formed by the lower (*geza*) side of the ro. With your hands resting slightly apart on your lap, sit there in waiting (115).

Once the second guest begins to drink the koicha, the first guest inquires about the name of the tea, the producer of the tea, the name and maker of the confection, and related points of interest.

Respond to the questions (116). When the last guest takes the last sip, shift your sitting position back to *imae* (117).

Undo the *nakajimai* as follows: Grasp the futaoki with your left hand (118), take it with your right hand, set it in your left palm, re-hold it from above with your right hand, and return it where it was to the right of the ro (119). Take the hishaku with your left hand and, while rotating that hand inward, bring the hishaku vertically in front of you.

Re-position the hishaku with your right hand, re-hold the handle with the left thumb and forefinger, and take the set hishaku posture.

With your right hand, remove the lid from the kettle (120), and set it on the futaoki (121). [Fukusa user: After taking the set hishaku posture, pick up the fukusa which rests beside your left knee with your right hand, and use it to remove the lid from the kettle. Then set it back down beside your left knee.] Hold the hishaku with your right hand as though to scoop hot water, rotate it so that the cup faces down, and rest the hishaku on the kettle in the standard manner for ro temae (122).

Take the chakin from the mizusashi lid with your right hand (123), and place it *tenari* on the kettle lid (124).

With your right hand, grasp the mizusashi lid handle (125), bring the lid toward you, transfer it to your left hand, which grasps it at about the halfway point between the left side and far side (126), and lean the lid against the left side of the mizusashi (127). The lid handle should be on the side facing the mizusashi.

Pick up the hishaku in the standard manner (128) and, as you rotate your hand inward to turn the hishaku cup upward, bring the hishaku over your knees and hold the handle near the node with your left thumb and forefinger. Slide your right fingers to the end of the handle, then swivel your right hand to hold the handle from underneath.

Continue to slide your right hand up the handle, to hold it for use (129). See "Taking the hishaku in order to draw water from the water jar," page 59, *Urasenke Tea Procedure Guidebook 1*. Scoop a ladleful of cold water from the mizusashi (130), pour it into the kettle (131), and immediately rest the hishaku on the kettle in the standard manner. [Fukusa user: After this, pick up the fukusa from the right side with your right hand, place it on your left palm flipped right to left so that the loose corners are on top, take the uppermost triangular corner with your right thumb and forefinger, and let the fukusa fall away from your left hand, so that it hangs from your right hand in the form of a large triangle. In

the standard manner, fold that into two, and tuck the fukusa into your obi. See "Hanging the fukusa from your obi" steps 4–10, pages 35–36, *Urasenke Tea Procedure Guidebook 1*.] Wait for the guests to conduct *haiken* of the chawan (and kobukusa) and for the first guest, together with the last guest, to then return it (them) to where you had originally set it (them) out (132).

If, after step 107, no kobukusa was placed out with the koicha, then when the chawan is returned and the first and last guests have returned to their seats, pick the chawan up with your right hand (133), rest it on your left palm, re-hold it from the side with your right hand (134), and place it in front of you (135). Here again is a bow between host and guests (*shukyaku sōrei*). Make a *sō* bow (136).

If, after step 107, you set out a kobukusa next to the chawan, then when they are returned, first take the kobukusa with your right hand from the right side with your thumb on top and fingers below and tuck it into the front fold of your kimono.

Take the hishaku from the kettle in the standard manner and immediately scoop hot water from the kettle (137). Pour the hot water into the chawan (138), and return the hishaku to the kettle (139). Pick up the chawan with your right hand, transfer it to your left hand, and empty the hot water into the kensui (140).

Return the chawan to its place in front of you with your right hand (141). Then make a *sō* bow and inform the first guest that you will conclude the temae ("Oshimai itashimasu") [Note: If koicha temae will be followed by usucha temae, say that you will conclude the temae for the moment, "Ichiō oshimai itashimasu"] (142).

Concluding the temae

Pick up the hishaku in the standard manner (143) and, as described for steps 128–129 on pages 94–95, hold it for use. Scoop water from the mizusashi (144).

Pour the water into the chawan (145), and return the hishaku to its place resting on the kettle in the standard manner (146).

Take the chasen with your right hand and conduct the simple version of *chasentōshi*, in which the chasen is only raised once to check the tines (147). Return the chasen to where it was (148). Take the chawan with your right hand, transfer it to your left hand, and empty the water into the kensui (149).

Take the chakin from the kettle lid with your right hand (150), set it in the chawan (151), re-hold the chawan with your right hand, and set it down in front of you (152). Take the chasen with your right hand and set it in the chawan, making sure that the knot of the thread at the base of its tines (*kagariito*) is facing upward (153).

Take the chashaku with your right hand (154), and, resting that hand lightly on your right thigh, hold the kensui with your left hand (155) and move it back and closer to the wall (156).

With your left hand, remove your fukusa from your obi (157). Adjust your right-hand hold on the chashaku to grasp it deep in your palm with your ring finger and little finger, and fold the fukusa for purifying the chashaku (158).

Readjust your right-hand hold on the chashaku, and conduct the simple version of purifying the chashaku, sliding the fukusa down it only twice (159). Place the chashaku on the chawan, scoop facing downward (160). Dust off the fukusa over the kensui (161). Then, follow the standard procedure to flip the folded fukusa over onto your left palm, open the fukusa into the large triangle shape, fold that into two, and tuck the fukusa into your obi (162).

Hold the chaire from the side with your right hand (163), and place it to the front right of the mizusashi (164). Pick up the chawan from the side with your right hand (165), re-hold it from the left side with your left hand (166), and with your left hand, place it to the left of the chaire in front of the mizusashi (167).

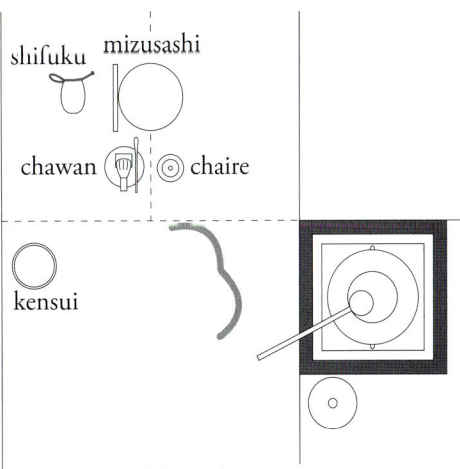

The positions of the implements when the chaire and chawan have been placed in front of the mizusashi (step 167)

Pick up the hishaku in the standard manner (168) and, as described in steps 128–129, pages 94–95, hold it for use to scoop cold water from the mizusashi. Scoop a ladleful of cold water from the mizusashi (169), and pour it into the kettle (170). Briefly hold the hishaku in front of you in the set hishaku pose, and then, with your right hand, set the kettle lid onto the kettle *tenari*, leaving it slightly ajar as it was at the start (171).

Rest the hishaku on the futaoki (172). With your left hand, grasp the mizusashi lid (173), move it toward you as you make it horizontal, grasp the handle with your right hand (174), and replace the lid onto the mizusashi (175).

Setting out the implements for *haiken*

At the point when you close the mizusashi lid, the first guest asks to do *haiken* of the chaire, chashaku, and shifuku. Acknowledge that request with a *sō* bow (176). [Note: Guests for koicha as a general rule always ask for *haiken*.] Pick up the hishaku with your right hand (177), bring it in front of you and re-hold it from under the handle around the node with your left hand (178), and set it on the kensui with your left hand (179) so that the cup is facing downward and hangs outside the kensui rim and the handle is parallel to the *kattetsuki* wall.

Take the futaoki from above with your right hand (180), transfer it to your left hand (181), and shift your sitting position to directly face the mizusashi (182).

Again hold the futaoki from above with your right hand, re-hold it from the side with your left hand, and set it behind the kensui, under the hishaku handle (183).

Pick up the chawan from the right-front with your right hand (184) and directly place it on the *kattetsuki* side of the temaeza (185).

Pick up the chaire from the side with your right hand, place it in your left palm (186), and, while holding your right hand over the front of your right knee to keep your kimono in place, shift your sitting position to sit facing the *kyakutsuki* side of the temaeza so that your body is centered with the lower edge of the ro frame (187). Set the chaire down in front of you with your right hand (188).

Take the fukusa from your obi, and fold it in the standard way, as though you are about to purify a natsume (189).

Pick up the chaire from the side with your left hand (190). In the same manner as done earlier in the temae to purify the chaire, wipe the lid's far and near surfaces as though writing the Chinese numeral "二" (191), press the fukusa against the body of the chaire and let the fukusa open one fold in your palm (192), and wipe the body by rotating the chaire counter-clockwise using your left fingers.

After making two full rotations, slide your right hand and the fukusa downwards off the chaire, and set the fukusa down in front of you (193). Remove the chaire lid with your right hand, glance at the underside of the lid (194), then set the lid down on the far side of the fukusa (195).

Immediately pick up the fukusa with your right hand (196), lightly press its top side against the body of the chaire, and re-grasp the fukusa so that it is folded back into its fully folded state (197). Wipe the far and near edges of the mouth of the chaire (198).

Set the fukusa on the tatami where it was a moment ago (199), and then immediately pick up the chaire lid (200).

111

Replace the chaire lid onto the chaire (201). Then, with your right hand, hold the chaire from the right side, place it on your left palm, turn it in two clockwise moves so that the front faces away from you (202), and set it in the corner of the ro tatami, at a point approximately one medium-sized natsume away from the tatami bordering and the ro frame (203). Pick up the fukusa with your right hand (204) and, in the standard manner, return it to your obi.

Shift your sitting position to once again face the mizusashi (205). Take the chashaku from the chawan with your right hand (206), and turn it so that the scoop faces upward as you transfer it to your left hand (207). Adjust your sitting position to return to *imae*; that is, the temae sitting position (208).

Re-hold the chashaku from above just below the node with your right thumb and forefinger so that the thumb comes to the right of the chashaku and the fingers are to its left (209), and set the chashaku down on the lower side (*geza*) of the chaire, its handle pointing towards the guests (210). See detailed images of the chashaku handling in *Urasenke Tea Procedure Guidebook 2*, page 41.

Pick up the shifuku with your left hand (211). Hold it from the right side with your right hand, and set it on your left palm (212). Adjust your sitting position to again sit facing the *kyakutsuki* side of the temaeza so that your body is centered with the lower edge of the ro frame (213). Place your right thumb on top of the base of the shifuku and fingers on the base, and set the shifuku on the *geza* side of the chashaku with its base toward the guests (214, 215).

Removing the tea implements

Shift your sitting position to once again face the mizusashi, and then take the hishaku from the kensui with your left hand (216, 217).

Bring the hishaku in front of you, and redirect its handle with your right hand so that the hishaku is horizontal and its cup is to the left and facing upward. Clench your right hand fingers around the hishaku handle at the node and hold the hishaku steady in that position (218). Pick up the futaoki from the side with your left hand (219), and grasp it from the top with your right thumb, forefinger, and middle finger (220).

Pick up the kensui with your left hand (221), and stand up leading with your left leg (222). Turn away from the guests, proceed to the sadōguchi, making all the tatami-to-tatami cross-overs with your left foot, and sit facing the closed sadōguchi.

Set the kensui down in front of your knees. Take the futaoki with your left hand and set it down to the right of the kensui. Hold the hishaku handle from underneath with your left thumb and first two fingers, then re-grasp the handle with your right hand so that you can turn the hishaku cup downward.

Rest the hishaku on the kensui so that it is parallel with the sadōguchi threshold and its downward-facing cup is hanging to the left outside the kensui rim (223). Open the sadōguchi fusuma. Then, in the reverse process of the manner in which you set the kensui, futaoki, and hishaku down, hold them as you were holding them before, stand from your left leg (224), step up to the threshold

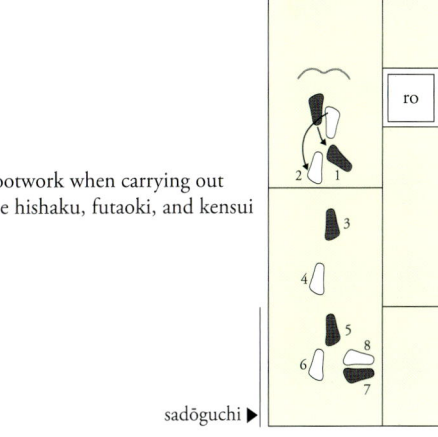

Footwork when carrying out the hishaku, futaoki, and kensui

sadōguchi ▶

with your right foot, and cross into the mizuya with your left foot.

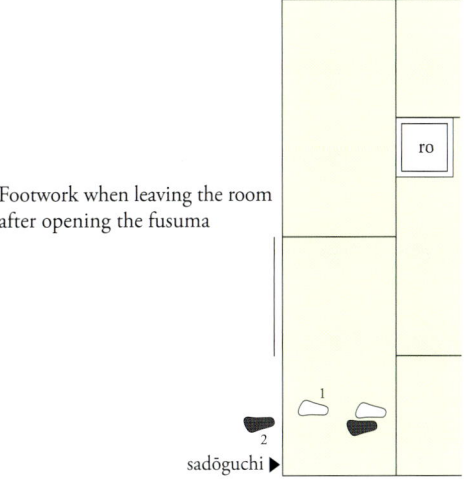

Footwork when leaving the room after opening the fusuma

sadōguchi ▶

Once the host goes to the mizuya with the kensui, the first guest goes to get the chaire, chashaku, and shifuku, and brings them back to his seat. See "*Haiken* of the Chaire, Chashaku, and Shifuku" steps 2–6, pages 139–141 herein.

Having set aside the kensui, futaoki, and hishaku in the mizuya, return to the temaeza and sit down facing the mizusashi. Pick up the chawan with your right hand (225), place it in your left palm, and steady it with your right hand. Stand up leading with your left foot, turn toward the guests, and take the chawan to the mizuya (226). Again return to the temaeza and sit down facing the mizusashi. Hold the mizusashi deeply with both hands (227), stand up, turn toward the guests as before, and take the mizusashi to the mizuya. Upon exiting, turn around to face the sadōguchi, sit down, set the mizusashi down in front of your knees, and close the fusuma (228).

Once the host closes the fusuma, the first guest does *tsugirei* to the next guest and starts the *haiken*. When all the guests in turn have finished their *haiken*, the last guest takes the items to the first guest, who comes forward to a spot near where the host set them out and there gets them from the last guest. The first guest then sets them back on the tatami adjacent to the temaedatami. (This procedure in which the first and last guests meet in order to return the items to the host is called *deai de kaesu*.) See "*Haiken* of the Chaire, Chashaku, and Shifuku" steps 7–18, pages 140–144 herein.

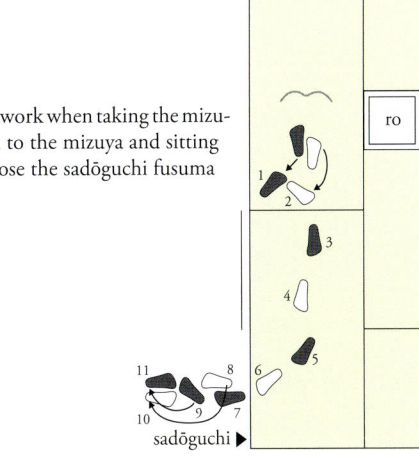

Footwork when taking the mizu-sashi to the mizuya and sitting to close the sadōguchi fusuma

Footwork when coming in and sitting to retrieve the *haiken* items

Retrieving the *haiken* items

Sit at the sadōguchi. When it seems that the *haiken* items have been returned, open the fusuma (229) and, once you have confirmed that the guests are settled back in their seats, stand from your right leg and proceed to the temaedatami, making all the tatami-to-tatami cross-overs with your right foot. Sit so that the *haiken* items are directly in front of you. The first guest thanks you with a bow. Return that bow. Then answer any questions about the items (230).

Take the shifuku from the base with your right hand (231). Place it on your left palm. Take the chashaku with your right hand (232). Rest it at an angle on top of the shifuku, and lightly hold it in place with your left thumb (233). Take the chaire from the side with your right hand (234).

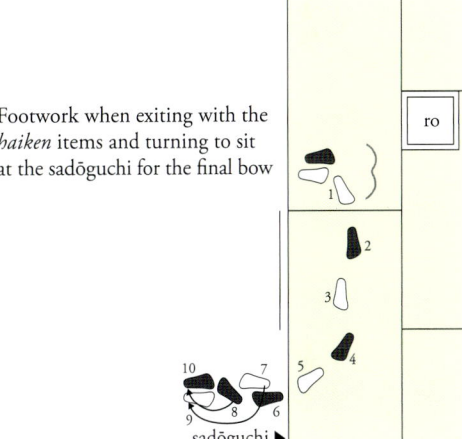

Footwork when exiting with the *haiken* items and turning to sit at the sadōguchi for the final bow

Holding the chaire and chashaku/shifuku in front of you, stand up leading with your left leg (235), then bring your right foot to the lower end of the temaedatami and return to the mizuya, making all the tatami-to-tatami cross-overs with your left foot (236). Upon entering the mizuya, turn around to face the sadōguchi, and sit down.

Set the chaire down close to your knee on the side toward the wall post (*tatetsuke*) (237). Take the chashaku with your right hand and set it next to the chaire on the side toward the wall post. IF the wall post is on your right, hold the shifuku from the right side with your right hand, and flip it over onto your left palm to bring the braided-together end of the shifuku cord to the left (the side which will be closer to the chaire) (238).

Take the shifuku from the base with your right hand and set it next to the chashaku (239). [IF the wall post is on your left, the shifuku need not be flipped over before you set it next to the chashaku; therefore, simply take the shifuku from the base with your right hand and immediately set it next to the chashaku. See Furo Koicha Temae step 213 and "Setting the shifuku down with the chaire and chashaku" note, page 60 herein.] Make a formal *shin* bow (240), and close the fusuma.

Knowledge for Guests

Partaking of Koicha

Haiken of the Chaire, Chashaku, and Shifuku

How to Partake of Confections Served in a Fuchidaka

Partaking of Koicha

A bowl of koicha contains servings for a number of guests. Each guest drinks approximately three-and-a-half sips, wipes the area of the bowl rim from where he/she drank, and then passes the bowl on. The host might prepare and set out kojakin (small chakin) or folded kaishi substitutes for the convenience of guests who are not prepared with their own kojakin to wipe the bowl rim; however, koicha guests should not expect this, and should be prepared with their own. The kojakin is prepared by moistening it slightly with water, folding it into thirds lengthwise, and then folding the resulting strip into fourths, to be kept in your water-proof kojakin-ire and stored within your kimono or fukusabasami.

Kojakin in Kojakin-ire

The following instructions for guests are based upon the premise that it is a furo temae and the tea room is an 8 tatami *hiroma* of conventional orientation. As for getting items from the host and returning them to the host in a *koma* (room no more than 4.5 tatami in floor space) or when the distance between yourself and your destination is less than what would amount to the length of a full tatami and could be crossed in less than four steps, the usual rule is to remain in the seiza position and move forward or backward by pressing your hands to the floor to scoot yourself (*nijiru*) in the desired direction. See "Getting and returning items in a small tea room," page 111, *Urasenke Tea Procedure Guidebook 2*.

If the chawan is Raku ware, and therefore the use of a kobukusa is not involved

The host sets out the chawan (1). The first guest, in the same manner that he would for usucha, stands up leading from his right leg (2), proceeds toward the chawan making all tatami-to-tatami cross-overs with his right foot, sits and picks up the chawan (3), holds it in the standard manner, stands up from his left leg, turns in the direction of the other guests, and returns to his seat, making all tatami-to-tatami cross-overs with his left foot (4). Once inside his space, he turns around in the direction of the other guests, and sits down.

Now, because this is koicha to be shared among the guests, the first guest places the chawan between himself and the next guest inside the tatami bordering (5), and all guests make a *shin* bow (6).

The first guest picks up the chawan with his right hand (7), places it in his left palm (8), and bows slightly while raising the chawan somewhat, in an expression of thankfulness (9). He rotates the chawan clockwise so that the front no longer faces him (10). He then takes a sip of the koicha (11). At this point, the host inquires about the quality of the koicha ("Ofukukagen wa?"). The first guest bows just with his right hand placed on the floor and responds that it is good ("Kekkō degozaimasu") (12). He takes about two-and-a-half more sips, keeping in mind the amount of tea and number of remaining guests. Around this timing, the second guest does *tsugirei* to the next guest, making a *gyō* bow and saying "Osaki ni," and that person responds with a *gyō* bow (13).

When the first guest finishes the three-and-a-half sips, he places the chawan in front of him inside the tatami bordering, takes out his prepared kojakin, wipes the part of the chawan rim from which he drank (14), puts the used kojakin away, and then picks up the chawan with his right hand, places it in his left palm, and rotates it counter-clockwise, returning the front to face him (15). He and the second guest move one knee's-breadth toward each other so as to diagonally face one another, and the first guest hands the chawan to the second guest (16).

The two return to their forward-facing positions, and then bow in unison, to acknowledge between them that the koicha has duly been passed along (*okuri-rei*) and received (*uke-rei*). For this, the first guest makes a *gyō* bow, while the second guest, holding the chawan, simply bows down slightly (17). After this, she follows the standard manners for guests before drinking matcha, and then begins to drink her portion of the koicha (18). Once the second guest takes a sip of the koicha, the first guest bows to the host, thanks him for the tea, and inquires about the name of the tea ("O-chamei wa?") and the producer of the tea ("O-tsume wa?"). It is also typical to thank the host for the confection served before the koicha and to ask about the confection's name and maker (19). Within the flow of a formal tea gathering, this is also an opportunity to ask about different aspects of the tea setting that were employed or have been changed since the partaking of the meal during the initial seating (*shoiri*), and other related points of interest. Meanwhile, the second guest finishes drinking her portion of the koicha, wipes the chawan rim, and hands the chawan to the next guest, who in this case is the last guest, in the same manner as did the first guest. They too do *okuri-rei* and *uke-rei* in unison. When the last guest finishes the last of the koicha and sets the chawan down to wipe the rim (20), the first guest asks the last guest for *haiken* of the chawan ("O-chawan no haiken o"). The last guest acknowledges this request (*uke-rei*) (21), and proceeds with wiping the chawan rim. He holds the chawan and, after returning the front to face himself (22), delivers the chawan to the first guest (23). [Depending upon the distance involved, he may stand up and walk to do this, or may remain seated and *nijiru* to do this. See "Getting and returning items in a small tea room," page 111, *Urasenke Tea Procedure Guidebook 2.*]

Before placing the chawan outside the tatami bordering in front of the first guest, the last guest, in the standard manner, rotates it clockwise so that it faces the first guest (23, 24). He then returns to his seat.

The first guest does *tsugirei* to the next guest ("Osaki ni"), and the next guest bows in acknowledgement (25). The first guest then places both hands on the tatami as in the *shin* bow position, and views the chawan in its entirety (26). He bends down, takes the chawan in his hands, rests his elbows lightly on his thighs, and examines the chawan's details, taking note also of the appearance of the koicha still adhering to its interior (27).

The first guest sets the chawan down outside the tatami bordering again, and once more views it in its entirety. Around this timing, the second guest does *tsugirei* to the third guest (28). Having finished his *haiken*, the first guest takes the chawan with his right hand and immediately places it between himself and the next guest, within the tatami bordering. The next guest takes the chawan with her right hand, sets it in front of herself outside the tatami bordering, and proceeds to do *haiken* of the chawan and finally pass it to the third guest in the same manner as did the first guest. The last guest does *haiken* of the chawan in the same manner (29). When the last guest finishes his *haiken* of the chawan, he places it to his lower side, within the bordering of his tatami (30). The last guest and first guest will meet by the place where the host placed the chawan out, in order to return it to the host, and so now they silently confirm with each other that they are ready to do so (31). Then the last guest picks up the chawan with his right hand, and because in this case he will walk to deliver the chawan, he holds it in the standard manner and stands up from his right leg. At this same time, the first guest also similarly stands up.

They both proceed toward where the first guest originally sat when he went to get the chawan, and they sit down; the first guest sitting where he can easily return the chawan, and the last guest in a position where he can place it out in front of the first guest. The last guest turns the chawan in his left palm so that the front faces the first guest, holds the chawan from the side with his right hand, and sets it in front of the first guest (32). The last guest then stands up from his left leg, turns in the direction of the first guest, and returns to his seat.

The first guest picks up the chawan with his right hand, transfers it to his left palm, turns it so that the front faces the opposite direction, then sets it where the host originally set it out, making sure that the front faces the temaeza (33). The first guest stands up from his left leg, turns in the direction of the other guests, and returns to his seat.

The host takes the chawan and places it in front of himself. Here is a bow between host and guests (*shukyaku sōrei*). All guests make a *shin* bow in unison (34).

When a kobukusa is set out with the chawan

In this section, the methods which are in common with if the chawan is Raku ware and therefore a kobukusa is not involved are abbreviated. Refer to the previous section for details of those basic methods.

If the chawan is not Raku ware, the host will set a kobukusa out next to it (1). In the standard manner, the first guest goes and sits where he can easily reach the items. He picks up the chawan with his right hand and places it on his left palm. He then picks up the kobukusa from the right side (the *wasa* side) with his thumb on top and fingers underneath, and supports the chawan from the side by holding the kobukusa upright along the right side of the chawan (2). Carrying the items in this manner, he returns to his seat (3).

Once in his seat, he places the kobukusa in the upper (*jōza*) corner inside the tatami bordering (4). He holds the chawan from the right side with his right hand, and places it between himself and the next guest inside the tatami bordering (5). All the guests make a *shin* bow in unison (*sōrei*).

The first guest takes the chawan with his right hand and places it in front of himself inside the tatami bordering. He says to the host that he will borrow the kobukusa ("Kobukusa haishaku itashimasu") (6).

He picks up the kobukusa with his right hand, places it in his left palm, and opens it out (7). Next, he picks up the chawan with his right hand, rests it on the kobukusa in his left palm, steadies the chawan from the side with his right hand, and bows slightly while raising the chawan somewhat, in an expression of thankfulness (8). He rotates the chawan twice so that the chawan front no longer faces him, taking care to lift the chawan up slightly from the kobukusa during each rotation, and then takes a sip of the koicha.

At this point, the host inquires about the quality of the koicha that he has prepared ("Ofukukagen wa?"). The first guest, keeping the chawan held carefully in his left palm, bows just with his right hand placed on the floor and responds that it is good ("Kekkō degozaimasu") (9). He finishes drinking his portion of the koicha, and, around this timing, the second guest does *tsugirei* to the next guest, making a *gyō* bow and saying "Osaki ni," and that person responds with a *gyō* bow.

The first guest, having finished drinking his portion of the koicha, uses his right and left hands to hold the chawan and kobukusa together from the right and left sides, and sets them down together in front of him inside the tatami bordering. He uses his prepared kojakin to wipe the part of the chawan rim from which he drank (10), puts away the used kojakin, and then picks up the chawan together with the kobukusa by holding them as he did when he set them down. Moving his left hand under the kobukusa to hold the kobukusa with chawan on it in his left palm as before, he then rotates the chawan twice counter-clockwise with his right hand in the standard manner, returning the front to face him. In the same manner as when a kobukusa is not involved, he hands the chawan to the second guest, but in this case, together with the kobukusa upon which it is resting. The two return to their forward-facing positions, and then conduct the *okuri-rei* and *uke-rei*, bowing in unison to acknowledge between them that the koicha has duly been passed along and received. Once the second guest begins to drink the koicha, the first guest thanks the host for the tea and inquires about the name of the tea, the producer of the tea, the confection, and so on.

kobukusa to the first guest. Sitting facing the first guest, he temporarily sets the kobukusa down by his side, and in the standard manner, rotates the chawan clockwise so that it faces the first guest before placing it in front of the first guest outside the tatami bordering. He then picks up the kobukusa, places it in his left palm, grasps it from the opposite side with thumb on top, and sets it to the lower (*geza*) side of the chawan with the folded (*wasa*) side to his left (the first guest's right) (16). [If he will remain seated and *nijiru* to do this, then after wiping the chawan rim at step 15, holding the chawan in his left palm, and returning the front to face himself, he sets it out some distance in the direction which he will go, takes the kobukusa with his right hand and sets it out to the lower (*geza*) side of the chawan, and scoots forward. He repeats this moving of the chawan, kobukusa, and himself until he is sitting facing the first guest.]

Meanwhile, the second guest finishes drinking her portion of the koicha, wipes the chawan rim, and hands the chawan together with kobukusa to the next guest, who in this case is the last guest, in the same manner as did the first guest (11). They too do *okuri-rei* and *uke-rei* in unison (12).

When the last guest finishes drinking the last bit of koicha, he takes just the chawan with his right hand and places it in front of himself within the tatami bordering (13), leaving the kobukusa in his left palm. He then folds the kobukusa in half from right to left with his right hand, grasps the right side (*wasa*) with his right hand with thumb on top, and sets it down to his lower side (*geza*) inside the tatami bordering (14). At this timing, the first guest asks the last guest for *haiken* of the chawan ("O-chawan no haiken o"). The last guest acknowledges this request (*uke-rei*), and then proceeds with wiping the chawan rim with his prepared kojakin (15) and then putting the used kojakin away. He then places the chawan in his left palm and returns the front to face himself.

If he will stand up and walk to deliver the chawan and kobukusa to the first guest, he now picks up the kobukusa and holds it upright along the right side of the chawan as did the first guest when originally getting the items. See step 2, page 133 herein. Carrying the items in this way, he delivers the chawan and

Once the last guest has returned to his seat, the first guest takes the kobukusa from the right side with his right hand and places it in the upper (*jōza*) corner inside the tatami bordering, then does *tsugirei* to the next guest, and conducts his *haiken* of the chawan. When he sets the chawan back down to finally view it in its entirety again, the second guest does *tsugirei* to the third guest. The first guest places the chawan between himself and the second guest within the tatami bordering, and then picks up the kobukusa with his right hand, places it in front of him outside the tatami bordering, and does *haiken* of it following the same steps as with the chawan (17). The second guest meanwhile conducts her *haiken* of the chawan. When the first guest finishes his *haiken* of the kobukusa, he takes it with his right hand from the right side (*wasa*) and places it between himself and the next guest as he did with the chawan, inside the tatami bordering.

The second guest follows the same pattern as did the first guest for conducting her *haiken* of both the chawan and kobukusa and passing them to the next guest.

The last guest does *haiken* of the chawan and kobukusa in the same manner as the others before him, placing the chawan to his lower side, within the bordering of his tatami bordering, when he is finished with its *haiken*, and placing the kobukusa further over to the lower side of the chawan when he is finished with its *haiken*. At this timing, the last guest and first guest silently confirm with each other that they are ready to meet by the place where the host set out the chawan and kobukusa, in order to return these items to the host. Then the last guest picks up the chawan with his right hand, and because in this case he will walk to deliver the chawan and kobukusa, he holds the chawan in his left palm, then picks up the kobukusa and holds it upright along the right side of the chawan as did the first guest when originally getting the items, and stands up from his right leg. At this same time, the first guest also similarly stands up. They both proceed toward where the first guest originally sat when he went to get the items, and they sit down; the first guest sitting where he can easily return the items, and the last guest in a position where he can place them out in front of the first guest. The last guest places them out to the first guest in the same manner that he did when he delivered them to him for *haiken* (18). The last guest then stands up from his left leg, turns in the direction of the first guest, and returns to his seat.

The first guest picks up the chawan with his right hand, transfers it to his left palm, then turns it so that the front faces the opposite direction, and sets it where the host originally set it out, making sure that the front faces the temaeza. He then picks up the kobukusa from the right side (the *wasa* should be on this side at this stage) with his right hand, places it in his left palm, re-holds it from the opposite side, and returns it to where the host originally placed it out, with its *wasa* now to the left (the host's right) (19). The first guest stands up from his left leg, turns in the direction of the other guests, and returns to his seat.

Haiken of the Chaire, Chashaku, and Shifuku

At the point in the koicha temae when the host closes the mizusashi lid (step 158, pages 46 and 47), the first guest asks to do *haiken* of the chaire, chashaku, and shifuku ("Chaire, chashaku, shifuku no haiken o") (1), and the host acknowledges this with a bow. The host continues to conclude the temae, and he sets the requested *haiken* items out for the first guest to come get them.

When the host exits into the mizuya with the kensui, the first guest proceeds toward the *haiken* items. He sits, picks up the shifuku from the base with his right hand, and transfers it to his left palm. He next picks up the chashaku with his right hand, places it at an angle on top of the shifuku, and lightly holds it in place with his left thumb. He takes the chaire from the side with his right hand (2), and then, holding the items in front of him, stands leading with his left foot, turns in the direction of the other guests, and returns to his seat. Once he is inside his space, he turns around in the direction of the other guests, and sits down. He places the chaire close to his upper side (*jōza*), within the bordering of the tatami on which he sits, leaving space for the other items to be placed on its upper side (3).

The first guest places the chashaku next to the chaire on the side opposite himself (4). With his right hand, he grasps the right side of the shifuku and flips it from right to left in his left palm (5). This is so that the braided-together end (*uchidome*) of the cord will be on the side closer to the chaire when he sets the shifuku down in the next step. See "Setting the shifuku down with the chaire and chashaku" on page 60 herein. He holds the base of the shifuku, and places the shifuku next to the chashaku (6). The first guest keeps the items with him like this until the host exists into the mizuya with the mizusashi and closes the fusuma. At that point when the host has closed the fusuma, the first guest does *tsugirei* to the second guest, making a *gyō* bow and saying "Osaki ni," and the second guest bows in acknowledgement (7).

With his right hand, the first guest places the chaire in front of himself outside the tatami bordering. He places both hands on the tatami as in the *shin* bow position, and views the chaire in its entirety (8). Around this timing, the second guest does *tsugirei* to the third guest in advance.

When doing *haiken*, the first guest bends down, rests his elbows lightly on his thighs, steadies the chaire with his left hand, removes the lid with his right hand, and then, handling the lid with both hands, examines its details (9). He sets the lid down to the right of the chaire, top facing upward. Again lightly resting his elbows on his thighs, and being careful, he examines the details of the chaire (10). He replaces the lid with his right hand while steadying the chaire with his left hand, and once more views the chaire in its entirety. He picks up the chaire from the side with his right hand and places it between himself and the second guest, within the tatami bordering (11).

Next, he takes the chashaku with his right hand and places it in front of himself outside the tatami bordering. In the same manner as with the chaire, he does *haiken* of the chashaku and then the shifuku. While he does *haiken* of the chashaku, the second guest does *haiken* of the chaire (12). Each item is passed to the next guest within the tatami bordering. The guests all successively examine the chaire, chashaku, and shifuku as did the first guest (13). When the last guest finishes his *haiken* of the chaire, he places it to his lower (*geza*) side, within the bordering of his tatami, and when he finishes his *haiken* of the chashaku, he places that to the lower side of the chaire with his right hand (14).

When he is done with *haiken* of the shifuku, he places it in his left palm, grasps the right side of the shifuku, and flips it from right to left in his left palm. He then holds the base of the shifuku, and places the shifuku next to the chashaku (15).

At this timing the last guest and first guest silently confirm with each other that they are ready to meet by the place where the host set out the *haiken* items, in order to return them to the host. Then the last guest picks up the shifuku from the base with his right hand, and places the shifuku on his left palm. He next picks up the chashaku with his right hand, places it at an angle on top of the shifuku, and lightly holds it in place with his left thumb. He takes the chaire from the side with his right hand, and then, holding the items in front of him, stands leading with his right leg. At this same time, the first guest also similarly stands up (16). They both proceed toward where the first guest originally sat when he went to get the items, and they sit down; the first guest sitting where he can easily return the items, and the last guest in a position where he can place them out in front of the first guest. The last guest sets the chaire, chashaku, and shifuku down in front of himself. He then places them from left to right (the first guest's right to left) in front of the first guest (17), handling each one as necessary in order to face it toward

the first guest, like the host did when setting the items out. See steps 179, 180 on page 31, and steps 184, 189 on pages 52–53 herein. Then the last guest stands up from his left leg, turns in the direction of the first guest, and returns to his seat.

The first guest returns the chaire, chashaku, and shifuku to the place where the host set them out, but sets them there from left to right (the host's right to left). For this, he places the chaire on his left palm and rotates it so that the front faces the opposite direction before setting it in the place where the shifuku was set out by the host. He then picks up the chashaku with his right hand, transfers it to his left hand in order to regrasp it with his right hand so that its handle points away from him, and sets it in the place where it was set out, handle pointing toward the temaedatami. He places the shifuku in his left palm, places his right thumb on top of the base and fingers on the base, and sets the shifuku in the place where the chaire was set out by the host, with its base toward the temaedatami (18). He stands up from his left leg, turns in the direction of the other guests, and returns to his seat.

When the host returns from the mizuya to the temaedatami and sits facing the *haiken* items, the first guest bows and thanks the host, the host returns that bow, and then the first guest asks about the items (19).

How to Partake of Confections Served in a Fuchidaka

The name "fuchidaka" for the formal containers used to serve the omogashi at a chaji literally means "high rim," deriving from the fact that each container fundamentally is a high-rimed version of the kind of individual meal tray (*oshiki*) used for the kaiseki meal. A set of these is called "*fuchidakajū*," indicating that it is a tiered set of stackable fuchidaka. A full set, which basically will serve five guests, consists in five of the containers and a single lid for the topmost container. Each container holds a single omogashi, so for three guests, as in the example in this guidebook, the host will use just three of the containers. The first guest's omogashi is in the bottommost container, and the last guest's is in the topmost one. The host will provide kuromoji (picks made of spicewood, for the guests' use in taking and eating the omogashi), one per guest, placing them on the lid that covers the topmost container.

Although the steps for the last guest differ somewhat because his is the last container, having on it the lid, the basic steps for the guests in getting their container and kuromoji and eating the omogashi are as follows: Hold the stack of fuchidaka toward the bottom at both sides with both hands, lift it up slightly, and bow slightly, in an expression of appreciation (1). Set the stack back down, leave the bottommost container as is, and together slightly lift and re-position the upper container(s) so that they rest slightly counter-clockwise atop the bottommost one (2).

Place a kuromoji into the bottommost container through the opening you have created at its upper front-right corner (3). Hold the remaining container(s) with both hands, and place them between yourself and the next guest outside the tatami border (4). Take out your pack of kaishi and set it in front of you inside the tatami border, *wasa* side toward you (5). Use the kuromoji to take and place the omogashi on your kaishi (6). Rest the kuromoji on your kaishi, in front of the omogashi.

Do *haiken* of the empty fuchidaka container (7), and place it between yourself and the next guest outside the tatami bordering. To eat the omogashi, pick up the kaishi and use the kuromoji (8).

Group procedure

The stack of fuchidaka is in front of the first guest. He does *tsugirei* to the second guest (1). He then follows steps 1–2 described in the previous section (2).

Around when the first guest places the upper containers between himself and the second guest, the second guest does *tsugirei* to the third guest (3).

The first and second guests respectively proceed with the next steps described in the previous section (4). The only remaining uppermost container, with the lid and one remaining kuromoji, comes to the last guest (5). Meanwhile, the first guest has done *haiken* of his empty fuchidaka container and placed it between himself and the second guest outside the tatami bordering.

The second guest, having finished her *haiken* of her empty container, sets it slightly to the left, places the first guest's in front of her outside the tatami bordering, and then sets hers on it. The last guest re-positions the fuchidaka lid so that it rests slightly counter-clockwise atop the fuchidaka, places the kuromoji in the fuchidaka, and then sets the lid to the left outside the tatami bordering (6). After taking the omogashi onto his kaishi and doing *haiken* of the empty container, he replaces the lid. He places this to his left outside the tatami bordering, places the stack of empty containers in front of him, and sets his lidded container on top of the stack (7). He sets his kaishi, on which rest his omogashi and kuromoji, to the side, and, in two clockwise turns, rotates the stack of fuchidaka so that it faces away from himself. He then sets the stack by the sadōguchi. Once the last guest is back at his seat, he and the other guests pick up their kaishi and partake of the omogashi (8).

Glossary

chaire 茶入
The small, lidded ceramic jar for the tea powder used during koicha temae. Traditionally, its lid is made of ivory. Integral to a chaire is its *shifuku*.

chamei 茶銘
The name that a particular green tea variety has been given. Conventionally, the name indicates the quality or grade of the tea, or the name of the plantation where it was grown, and so forth. Nowadays, individuals such as priests and head masters of chanoyu traditions often give poetic names to particular green tea varieties, and these are described as "gamei" (雅銘), graceful names. Not to be mistaken with the word "chamei" written 茶名; the "tea name" given by the head master of a chanoyu tradition to a disciple.

deai de kaesu 出会いで返す
The act, at the end of the guests' *haiken*, of the first and last guest mutually coming forward and meeting in order for the last guest to pass the *haiken* items back to the first guest and the first guest to then set them in their prescribed places on the tatami adjacent to the temaedatami, for the host to retrieve them.

fuchidaka 縁高
The container formally used for serving the omogashi confection which precedes koicha. Properly called *fuchidaka-jū*. "*Fuchidaka*" literally means "high rim"; "*jū*" indicates "tiered." One set, for serving five guests, consists of five stacked square boxes and a lid.

fukukagen 服加減
The balance of the prepared usucha or koicha. This covers the ratio of the matcha powder to the hot water, the skillfulness with which they have been whipped or blended together, as well as the heat of the finished preparation.

geza (shimoza) 下座
The 'low seat'. This is the location countering the 'high seat' in a Japanese-style room where guests are received. Generally, the part of the room having the host's doorway is considered to be *geza*.

haiken 拝見
Respectful viewing. Term for the guests' studious viewing of the articles displayed in the alcove and at the dōgudatami, and of implements used in the temae. The guests do not touch the articles displayed in the alcove or at the dōgudatami when they do *haiken* of them, but may take the chaire, chashaku, and such temae items in hand to closely inspect their details. It is for the first guest to request to the host to be allowed to do *haiken* of such items employed in temae. The general etiquette is that the host offers these temae items out for *haiken* after being so requested.

heriuchi/herisoto 縁内・縁外
Terms indicating the position of something in relation to the tatami border (*heri*), from the perspective of the person sitting on the tatami. "Heriuchi" means "inside the border"; "herisoto" means "outside the border."

imae 居前
The host's prescribed sitting position at the temaeza for conducting the temae.

izumai 居ずまい
A person's form/appearance when seated. Toward the beginning of a chanoyu temae, there is a step for the host to make sure his/her clothing is not in disarray, and then pause in the proper sitting position for a moment of concentration. The phrase for this act is "*izumai o tadasu*," to straighten up one's form/appearance.

jōza (kamiza) 上座
The 'high seat'. The tokonoma is considered the highest place in a Japanese-style room, so the space in front of it is considered *jōza*. The main guest conventionally sits at or closest to this place. The contrasting 'low seat' location in the room is called *geza* (*shimoza*).

kattetsuki 勝手付き
The side of the temaedatami that is closer to the mizuya and further from the guests. In tea rooms of conventional orientation (*hongatte*), it is the left-hand side of that tatami.

kyakutsuki 客付き
The side of the temaedatami which is nearer to the guests and further from the mizuya. In tea rooms of conventional orientation (*hongatte*), it is the right-hand side of that tatami.

nakabuta 中蓋
Midpoint lid closure. The act of closing the opened lid of the kettle during the early part of a ro koicha temae once the hot water has been poured into the chawan to conduct the *chasentōshi*, to keep the kettle water well heated.

nakajimai 中仕舞い
1) The "midpoint closure" style of implement positioning when the temae is being brought to a close. It may be used instead of the "conventional closure" (*honjimai*) style for certain furo temae in *hiroma* tea rooms, mainly the basic ones. For *nakajimai*, the host sets the chawan and tea container so that they evenly straddle the imaginary left-right center line of the temaeza, rather than at their original locations in front of the mizusashi. 2) The "midpoint closure" procedure conducted during a ro koicha temae, in which the host, after confirming with the first guest that the koicha is satisfactory, closes the kettle lid, temporarily sets the hishaku and futaoki aside, and then sits in waiting as the guests drink the koicha.

nibiki 二引き
Lit., "draw 二." (ni, the kanji character for the numeral 2). Term used to describe the wiping of the lid of a container, such as a chaire, usuchaki, or mizusashi, in two left-to-right parallel horizontal strokes.

okuri-rei 送り礼
A bow made by a person who has sent along/passed along (*okuri*) something. It is made at the time of the transaction. The person who received the item simultaneously responds with an *uke-rei* bow. See uke-rei.

omogashi 主菓子
Lit., "main confection(s)." The relatively large and moist confections conventionally served with koicha, one per guest. As opposed to this, relatively small and dry confections referred to as *higashi* are conventionally served with usucha.

oshimai お仕舞い
Lit., "closing." The process of putting the implements away and concluding the temae.

shifuku 仕覆
A cloth pouch for items such as chaire, usuchaki, chawan, etc. Often made of distinguished historical textile (*meibutsugire*).

shikiita 敷板
General term referring to a board upon which something is placed. The size and type will depend upon its intended use. In chanoyu, the term is conventionally used to refer to the board upon which the furo is rested in the tea room.

sōrei 総礼
All-together bow. A bow made simultaneous by everyone. When the guests conduct *sōrei* in response to a bow from the host (*teishu*), it is called *shukyaku sōrei*, a simultaneous bow between host and guest(s).

sotozumi 外隅
See uchizumi.

tatetsuke 建付け
The wall post at the side of a sliding door panel such as a fusuma, which the door panel hits when it is slid shut.

teishu 亭主
Host. Conventionally, the person who conducts the temae. In a wider sense, the person who is presenting the hospitality.

teiza 定座
Lit., "standard seat." General term meaning the normal, prescribed spot where a person sits or a thing is set.

tenari 手なり
Lit., "as the hand would have it." A term to describe a natural manner of hand motion or direction of the hand when handling or setting down implements. This generally means movements or positions which are in alignment with your hand and arm position and which therefore do not cause you to bend your arm or wrist unnaturally.

tsugirei (jirei) 次礼
The courtesy expressed by a guest who is preceding the next guest in doing something, such as taking a confection, drinking tea, doing *haiken* of something, etc. The spoken words are, "Osaki ni," meaning, "Excuse me for going before you."

tsume 詰
1) The guest who is in the last seat; that is, the last guest (*makkyaku*). 2) Term used to indicate the expert tea producer (*chashi*) who manufactured/packed the leaf tea. During the koicha drinking by a group of guests, the first guest inquires to the host about the name of the tea's producer ("Otsume wa?").

uchizumi 内隅
Lit., "inner corner." This refers to the inner corner of the ro frame (*robuchi*). The "outer corner" is called *sotozumi*. These corners of the ro frame joint that is nearest the *dōgudatami* are used in ro temae as aiming points for the host's prescribed sitting position at the temaeza (*imae*).

uke-rei 受け礼
A bow made by someone who has just then received (*uke*) something. The "something" may be a concrete item, or it may be a request. The bow is made immediately when the item or request is received, to the person who relayed it.

wasa わさ
Lit., "loop." 1) The folded side of a kobukusa or piece/pack of kaishi that is in its usual folded-in-half state. 2) The doubled-over edge of a double-layer item made of textile, such as a fukusa or kobukusa. In the case of a fukusa or kobukusa, the other three edges are sewn together in an invisible fashion. 3) The looped part of a shifuku cord opposite the *uchidome*, the ends of the cord which are braided together.

yohōsabaki 四方捌き
The "four sided" (*yohō*) procedure for handling the fukusa during a koicha temae when the fukusa is about to be used to wipe and purify the chaire. Once the four sides of the fukusa are inspected, the fukusa is folded into its usual form for purifying a natsume, to begin the purifying of the chaire. This combination of techniques is called *sō-no-yohōsabaki*, the 'informal' (*sō*) four sided procedure.

Urasenke Tea Procedure Guidebook 3
Koicha Tea Procedure

［英文］裏千家茶道 点前教則 三

濃茶点前　風炉・炉

2019年4月3日　初版発行

著者	一般財団法人 今日庵理事長　千 宗室
翻訳	一般社団法人 茶道裏千家淡交会総本部国際部
	（グレッチェン・ミトワ　マイケル・ハーディ）
写真	宮野正喜
協力	大道雪代 (p.124 上写真)　中川未子 (p.6 下・囲みイラスト)
	マイケル・ハーディ (p.6 右列及び p.21 イラスト)
発行者	納屋嘉人
発行所	株式会社 淡交社
	本社 〒603-8588 京都市北区堀川通鞍馬口上ル
	営業 Tel.075-432-5151　編集 Tel.075-432-5161
	支社 〒162-0061 東京都新宿区市谷柳町39-1
	営業 Tel.03-5269-7941　編集 Tel.03-5269-1691
	www.tankosha.co.jp
装訂	株式会社 ザイン
印刷・製本	大日本印刷株式会社

©2019 一般財団法人 今日庵理事長　千 宗室
Printed in Japan　ISBN978-4-473-04290-3

定価はカバーに表示してあります。
落丁・乱丁本がございましたら、小社「出版営業部」宛にお送りください。
送料小社負担にてお取り替えいたします。
本書のスキャン、デジタル化等の無断複写は、著作権法上での例外を除き禁じられています。
また、本書を代行業者等の第三者に依頼してスキャンやデジタル化することは、
いかなる場合も著作権法違反となります。